AWAKEN

The Secret Science Of Spiritual Warfare

By

TC Carrier

[PLEASE REPEAT AFFIRMATION
EVERYTIME YOU BEGIN READING]

"I leave my ego at the door and open my heart in humility. Although I hear with my ears I will listen with my heart. I empty my cup ready to receive, as you can't fill a cup that is already full. I will have the open mind of a child and open to infinite possibilities beyond my understanding. I will not consider myself an expert on any subject, as I will stunt my own growth in the learning process. What impresses me the most about myself is how little I know. Vulnerability is my strength and I am ready to receive."

Printed in the United States of America.

First Edition.

ISBN # 978-0-9834462-9-3

House of Sacred Harmony Publishing
Website: www.TCCarrier.com

TABLE OF CONTENTS

INTRODUCTION

My family has a dog that I named after the Kemetic god, Anpu. We call her Pu for short. She is a small, black Chihuahua/Terrier mix. The god Anpu, who she is named after, leads us by the left hand in the afterlife so that we can find our way to the gates of heaven after we transition from this world. The ancients picked a black jackal to represent this god because this canine has unique characteristics that we need to understand regarding defining and navigating our souls in the spiritual realm. First off, Anpu takes our left hand because the left side of our body is controlled by the right hemisphere of our brain. It is the right hemisphere of our brain that knows the physical realm is an illusion. It does not define you or the world we live in according to our five senses which can be programmed. Also, it does not adhere to the laws and physics of this physical dimension. Thus, it is creative beyond our wildest imagination. It is spatial and infinite. It is artistic and has no boundaries or limitations. It is the right brain that leads us in the spiritual realm. It is these qualities that we need to home in on and nurture in an effort in reaching higher levels of spiritual consciousness. There is no coincidence that our hearts are also located on the left side of our bodies. This is what the term means to, "follow our hearts!"

What are the characteristics of the dog/god, Anpu that we need to pay attention to teach higher levels of consciousness? First off, dogs have night vision. They can see things in the dark that the human eye cannot detect. This tells us that seeing with our eyes is not to be believed in this realm. Our eyes are flawed in this dimension and can only detect a sliver of energy called the light spectrum which makes up a small fraction of all energy in this realm of existence, (less than 1% of all energy.) There is a higher realm that our human eyes cannot envision. Our "eyes" are useless in higher realms of consciousness and thus should not be trusted without having discernment while we are here. The saying, "Seeing is believing." It is not an accurate statement. We have a Pineal gland in between the two hemispheres of our brain at the level of the middle of our foreheads which our ancient, Kemetic ancestors called, "The First Eye." It is this gland that produces a chemical called Melanin, that when activated allows us to "see" in higher, spiritual realms, beyond the illusion of the physical dimension. It is a black substance just like the color of the Kemetic god Anpu. It is responsible for our intuition, discernment, anticipation, awareness, dream state and sixth sense. It allows us to see music, taste colors, feel emotions and smell in our dreams. It is these characteristics that we need to nurture and home in on in order to move into higher level of consciousness. This gland when maintained and tuned allowed our ancestors to see energy/spirit beyond our five senses. Thus, allow them to communicate and decipher energy at a much more advanced state that remains a mystery today. This allowed them access to higher realms of technology housed in the right brain and they didn't rely on the left brain which has limitations on the knowledge it can obtain, because it can only decipher information in the vacuum of the physical realm.

Dogs can also smell scents that the human nose cannot detect. The nose has the easiest access to the brain. This is why our ancestors performed brain surgery through the nasal passage. Our sense of smell is the strongest out of all our senses that invokes memory attached to emotions we call Nostalgia. To subtly manipulate one's consciousness, you would use their sense of smell to control what you want them to remember as well as what you want them to forget. If smells can spark nostalgia, they can also aid in suggestive memory loss like Alzheimer's or Dementia. This sense is unreliable in higher realms of consciousness as well. It is useless and one cannot take it with them. Dogs can also hear sounds and detect vibrations and frequencies that humans cannot. Again, proof that our physical dimension is not always what it seems to be and must not be trusted or fully invested in if you want to reach higher levels of consciousness. What sounds and frequencies are mainly in our music and media are we being infiltrated in to produce a desired effect on us by people who do not have our best interests? Sounds can heal. Sounds can inspire. Sounds can also kill. Sounds can also destroy. Sounds can promote fear and other sounds can inspire love. Sound is being used as a weapon to keep us at lower states of consciousness. Especially sounds that are undetectable to our naked ears.

The things dogs can teach us in our spirituality are a keen sense of awareness of things outside of our five senses, prudence, humility, thirst for knowledge and trusting our intuition. The Bible says, walk by faith and not by sight. This is what is meant when conscious people say and suggest that we are living in an illusion. The physical realm is literally made up of 99% empty space inside the atom, which is the basic building block of physical dimension. That empty voided space is filled with conditioning and programming that we are forced fed from the time our spirits incarnate into this physical dimension at birth. The things we "know" are real to us are never questioned because of our lifelong and relentless conditioning and programming on how we define ourselves and our environment that manipulates our definition of our reality.

Our pet dog Pu recently gave birth to a single, cute puppy we named, Oshun. The Orisha goddess of Love. When Oshun became old enough, I would take them in the backyard on the grass. I would then sprinkle tiny treats all around the yard for them to find, like an Easter egg hunt. The first four weeks, Mama Pu would find 95% of the treats and her puppy Oshun would only find 5%. This was because Pu was relying on her strongest ally, her sense of smell to track down and find tasty treats. Pu knew that her greatest asset was her ability to detect smells to decipher her reality and not being deceived by her eyesight, which was a weakness and can be fooled. On the other hand, the young Oshun was relying on her vision to find her treats, thus doing herself a disservice because her sense of smell was not fully developed yet and she didn't trust it. Her vision could not compare to her mother's sense of smell. As the puppy Oshun grew older, I could see her way of deciphering her reality shifted. She was now relying on her sense of smell over her sense of sight. Pretty soon Oshun was finding more treats than her mother! We humans must also shift how we define our reality by not relying on our five senses which can be deceiving and programmed to work against us, especially our sight. Although, seeing may be believing, what we believe may not necessarily be the truth. We need to nurture and trust our "First Eye" by defining ourselves and our reality according to our higher selves. This means not investing in the illusion, having no fear, showing humility, suppressing our Ego, always seek truth, open our heart, no boundaries, no limitations, a heightened sense of awareness, trusting your intuition and always follow our heart's intelligence! As the character Yoda in the movie Star Wars told his young, Jedi apprentice, Luke Skywalker, "You must unlearn what you have learned." This is what it means to walk by faith and not by sight. Having faith in your senses connected to your heart's intelligence and right brain and not what you have been brainwashed to believe is true. This is why recognizing and suppressing the Ego is crucial to reaching higher levels of consciousness. You must admit that you have been duped and scammed your whole life to start seeing the truth. This is what the Matrix relates to as "Taking the Red Pill."

CHAPTER ONE

Out Of Kemet, I Call My Son

People ask me all the time where do I get this unique information from and what started me down this rabbit hole searching for truth and freedom? I believe I was given unique circumstances in my DNA lineage and the environment I was raised in, that paved the way for me to follow my heart searching for the answer to one simple question, "Who am I?' Believe it or not, around the age of 8 years old, I would repeatedly ask myself this question repeatedly for hours at a time. It got so intense that I would lose myself and exit my physical body. I would be in my shadow self, staring back at my body like I was looking in the mirror, repeatedly asking this question to myself, "Who am I?" It got so intense that over time I feared my spirit body would not be able to find its way back into my physical body. The only thing that tethered my spirit to this physical dimension was my physical body. I believed without it, I would float into the dark abyss of the unknown never to return. This was the game I played throughout my childhood. How long and how far can I stay outside my physical body before my spirit body has to return? Over time, I got better at it and now as an adult, I can astral project almost instantly with little effort. But the strongest portal I can open in the spiritual dimension as an adult, while doing this exercise is, immediately before a sexual orgasm. But I digress as this exercise will be in a future book, lecture and/or class.

I was born of the conscious state of California to a Black father from South Central Los Angeles and a mother of mixed race, having a native indigenous mother from Mexico and a father of Southeast Asian descent. This was in the sixties where Black revolution was fervently in the air around the world. You had the assassinations of Medgar Evers, Martin Luther King, Malcolm X, Fred Hampton, Bobby Hutton, Emmitt Till, Patrice Lumumba, Che Guevara, Mehdi Ben Barka, Felix Moumie, Sylvanus Olympio, Eduardo Mondlane, John F. Kennedy, James Chaney, Andrew Goodman, Michael Schwerner, Robert F' Kennedy, and the dismantlement of the Black Panther Party to name a few. My father abandoned me soon after I was born and we moved to poor white "trash" neighborhoods soon thereafter. My mother never dared to mention my father to me, and she never told me I was of different ethnicity, as she didn't want to remember the pain she suffered at the hands of my Black father. Soon after this, my mother only dated red neck, racist, white men mainly from the deep south seemingly to get away from my Black father's stereotypical features. Little did she know, these brutally, racist men, would abuse her more than my father ever could. Unfortunately, I was ill-prepared for what was waiting for me once I started elementary school as the only Black kid in a poor, white institution. They brutally hammered me with racial taunts, slurs and physical abuse! They relentlessly, were determined to, "keep me in my place," as if their lives depended on it! I was at their mercy with no one to turn to. When I complained to my mother for support and protection, all she would tell me was to ignore them. She never even acknowledges that she had a Black son. Even my teachers would get into the act calling me racial slurs but at the time I was too naïve to know they were making fun and disrespecting me. I vividly remember one of my teachers calling me the name, "Bosco" throughout the whole school year. Finally, at the end of the year I asked my mother what that name meant. She told me it's chocolate syrup and asked me why I wanted to know. I told her and her red neck husband that my teacher called me that in class every day. They both laughed hysterically at one another and in the future, I would hear them tell that story to friends and co-workers and they would all laugh at my expense. From that day on, at the tender age of seven years old, I knew I was on my own with no one to protect or support me on my life's journey. I realized that all I can count on is me so "we" better suck it up and figure out how we were going to survive in this racial gauntlet I found myself in, with no escape in sight.

I soon started to figure things out. It was impossible for me to disappear as everywhere I turned I stood out like a sore thumb. If I couldn't hide, I could make myself as small as I could possibly be. That was my mission in life. I would sit slumping in the back of all my classes. I would never raise my hand to answer any questions even though I was very intelligent. I would not say one word to anybody throughout the whole day. I would eat and play by myself at lunch and at recess, finding the most remote locations on the school grounds. I would not look anybody in the eye when I walked down the hallways. My head was constantly fixed to peer at the ground wherever I went. This was my plan and it worked! This strategy did not eliminate the abuse, but it curtailed a big portion of it. This also trained my keen observation skills. I had to hone them in as my life depended on me being conscious of my surroundings. I learned to scan the area I was entering without others detecting it through my peripheral vision and minimal head movements. This attribute I mastered served me well later as I got into sports where awareness, subtle movements, intuition and anticipation make a great athlete!

As I got older and started climbing into higher grades, I observed one thing that was peculiar. Although, these white people let it be known that I wasn't welcomed around them, I did notice they gave Black athletes and Black celebrities a pass! They admired these Black people and seemed to accept them with open arms. This was shocking to me but at the same time I knew this was the path I had to take to survive in this world and have peace of mind. That day, I vowed to become the best athlete that I could be. When football season hit, I practiced night and day and became the best in the school! Soon after that basketball season started. You guessed it, I worked tirelessly to become the best basketball player in the school. When basketball season ended, it was time for track and field followed by the baseball season. I learned to dominate these sports as well. By the time I got to high school, these white people were cheering for me, wanted to be my friend, giving me things and going out their way to make my life easier. Even the teachers got into the act. I barely had to attend their classes, and they would still give me passing grades. I found my "white supremacy hack" and it was simple, become a star athlete! Become a celebrity! Coincidently, let this be a cautionary tale to all of us who look up to celebrities and put them on a pedestal. They are usually broken people with unresolved issues that they have never addressed. This is why they go so hard in their respective crafts even at a psychotic, dysfunctional and unhealthy desire to succeed and rise to the top, by any means necessary. Some even "sell their souls" to attain celebrity status. It is their unresolved pain that motivates them. It is their dysfunctional traumas and low self-esteem induced depression that drives them. When they make it to the top, they have been groomed and know how to speak the part. They looked the part and they acted very well. But what we must realize is that portion of them that we get a glimpse of, is just a "small portion" of them. It is a character they now play. The rest of the parts or pieces of them are broken thus, their trauma is never addressed and unresolved because of the fanatics that worship them unconditionally and the lavish lifestyles they hide behind. These celebrities literally suffer in silence. Please be careful what you wish for. This is a main reason why they turn to gluttony, drugs, deviant sexual activities and suicidal lifestyles to self-medicate and take the pain away. The celebrity thought that once they "made it" all their problems would disappear. Unfortunately, the opposite happens. All your problems you never addressed. All your insecurities, dysfunctions and traumas you never healed from are now magnified tenfold, while you surrounded by people telling you how great you are! Leaving them with no plan to escape or way to address these dysfunctions or even make them known. The celebrity becomes trapped in the illusion of their "egos" they embraced to achieve their fame and riches, while the other broken parts of them slowly fester as the spotlight no longer shines on them and the audience abandons them.

Playing sports at a high level led me to college as a student athlete. I started at the University of New Mexico and eventually transferred to San Francisco State University to play football. Little did I know this college was the first institution of higher learning to implement a Black Studies Department. People died in protests and strikes for this department to be at this University. Because it was the first Ethnics Studies Dept. of its kind, they built a "Dream Team" of college professors and scholars to man the department. Unbeknownst to me, this department would change my life trajectory forever. A funny thing happened on my way to playing in the NFL, marrying a white woman and living with my riches in a big mansion with luxury cars. I got conscious! The head football coach told me to take a Black studies course because the teacher looked out for Black athletes and it is an easy A. I signed up with the intention of sleeping in the back of the class and cruising to the end of the semester. My ears perked up when I heard stories of the middle passage and slavery, the properties of Melanin, the system of white supremacy, African spiritualty, great African civilizations, Black inventors and great Black revolutionaries! I was hooked! It got so bad for me that I would sit in Black studies courses I wasn't enrolled in and not attend the other classes I was officially enrolled in! I couldn't get enough information to satisfy my hunger for truth. I was lectured by master teacher scholars such as: Dr. Wade Nobles, Oba T'Shaka, Dr. Obenga, Francis Cress Welsing, Dr. Richard King, Neely Fuller, Nathan and Julia Hare to name a few! It was an all-star cast of Black scholars. By the time my senior year rolled around, my upper echelon, advanced classes had arrived covering an ancient Black civilization called, Kemet, otherwise known as, present day Egypt. This civilization and all its metaphysics and spiritual modalities opened me up to a cosmological and Universal holistic view of all the sciences and philosophies. In fact, this is now the basis of all the information that I decipher and interpret in all my books and lectures. For the first time in my life, I finally felt at home. I felt validated. I felt accepted. I could say I loved myself for the first time in my life.

One of my pitstops before I graduated college, was attending Catholic school at about 11 years of age. This was my introduction to my indoctrination into religious dogma. This experience also helped me in my spiritual awakening as I reminisce on my experience there. I was forced to learn all the books of the Bible and numerous Bible stories and parables. I read the Bible from front to back on two occasions. At 11 years old, I asked the priest for a meeting to ask a question that I could not wrap my head around. He called me into his office, and I proceeded to ask my perplexing question that haunted me. "Father, please help me understand." "Yes, my son," he replied. "What is your question?" "If a non-Christian, African man in a remote village sees a school bus fly over a cliff and plunge into a lake and he jumps in the lake and saves all the children in the bus and dies in the process. Does he go to heaven?" I anxiously inquired. The priest replied without hesitation. "No, my son. If he did not accept the Lord thy god as his Savior and Jesus as his Son who died on the cross for his sins, he would not be allowed in." In a state of confusion, I asked the priest my second question. "Ok, what if there was a serial killer who raped and killed 50 children and just before he was going to be executed, he shouts out that he accepts the Lord thy god as his Savior and Jesus died for his sins. Does he get to go to heaven?" The priest responds with conviction, "Of course my son, God our Father will welcome him with open arms!" "But why?" I protested. "It doesn't seem fair!" The father replied, "Sometimes it is not for us to understand but to keep our faith in the Lord. The Lord thy God works in mysterious ways, my son." After this conversation with the Catholic priest, I knew my spiritual journey to enlightenment would not be found in the church.

I am eternally grateful for my time at this strict and disciplined, Catholic school about my journey. This institution got me personally acquainted to the characters, parables, etymology, history and numerology that the Bible codes reveal. I learned that the literal translation of the Bible was the lowest level of conscious of understanding it. The Bible was coded and had deep hidden meanings. This Book needed to be cracked open and dissected metaphysically. The deeper the consciousness of the observer, the deeper the understanding the Bible revealed to you. The Bible meant different things to different readers based on the level of consciousness of the reader. One hundred people can interpret the Bible with 100 different meanings, and they all would be exact and correct according to the level of their consciousness and understanding. It's like asking a kindergartener what color the sky is? If he told you the answer was blue, you would say he is correct. If you ask a junior high student in science class the same question, he might say the sky is not blue. Blue having the shortest wavelength of all the colors in the light spectrum dominates our vision when we look at the sky. He would also be correct. If you ask a high school student in Physics class the same question, he might answer differently as well. The sky is not actually blue, but we are seeing the sun rays bouncing off the particles in our atmosphere to create the illusion of a blue sky. And if you were to ask a college professor specializing in quantum physics, he may give you another different answer according to his level of consciousness and understanding. All definitions of the color of the sky, and all interpretations of the Bible are exact and correct according to the consciousness of the observer.

One story in the Bible was like an epiphany to me when I read it. This story was my life story. Our lives seem to parallel each other in experiences, life lessons and clarity of our life's purpose. It was the story of Moses. Let's examine the parallels of our lives. The story goes that Pharaoh ordered all the young boys aged 2 and under to be murdered for fear of a savior being born to overturn him. Moses' mother, in a desperate attempt to save her son, put her baby in a basket, placed him in the Nile River hoping he would land somewhere safe so he could be saved. My father abandoned me as well. My mother took me out of the ghetto to a poor, white neighborhood where she thought I would be safe. Moses was taken in by the Pharaoh's daughter and raised like her own child where he learned the ways and the culture from the same people who were trying to kill him and enslave his people. I was also taken into the white community, who has a history of enslaving and oppressing Black people. While I was in their midst, I also learned their ways and culture. Moses grew up to use the Pharaoh's "magic" against him to free his people from bondage. My educational journey also led me to Kemet, which is the foundation for my philosophy and knowledge. I am also using the "Pharaoh's magic" to free my people. Since I lived with my enemy, went to school with them, befriended them, celebrated with them and collaborated with them, I have a unique and invaluable insight to their culture, beliefs and philosophies that Black people will never get a chance to experience without prejudice. Also, because I was raised outside of the Black community, I was never exposed to the generational programming and conditioning that our dysfunctional and traumatized, Black parents pass on to us without knowing it. The indoctrination of self-hate, colorism, use of the N word, impoverished mentality, crabs in a barrel mentality, drug and pimp culture, gang culture, sub-standard education, health care and nutrition, police brutality, violence & trauma, oversexualization and the like. When you combine all these factors in my life as I believe there are no coincidences, I realize that I have been groomed and chosen for this assignment that involves the resurrection and emancipation of my people. Moses was reluctant to embark on the journey that God chose him for. He fought with God and did not believe in himself. He even told God that his brother Aaron was more suitable for the task of freeing his people. It has also taken me a while to embrace this assignment I was given, as I did not seem worthy or qualified to take on such a monumental task. In fact. to this day some people even question if I am "Black" enough!

"When Herod saw that he had been tricked by the wise men, * he was infuriated, and he sent and killed all the children in and around Bethlehem who were two years old or under, according to the time that he had learned from the wise men."

-Matthew 2:16

As we grow older, hopefully we realize why we went through the difficulties of our childhood and moreover our not-too distant past. Each perceived hardship, abuse, trauma and overall uncomfortable life experiences taught us a unique characteristic about ourselves and our place in the world around us. One sign of knowing that we have healed from these traumas is recognizing they weren't losses in our lives but valuable lessons that we needed to learn to follow our hearts in seeking self-actualization or our life's purpose. These so-called "unfortunate circumstances" were required for us to correct a behavior or dysfunctional thought process we may have unknowingly had that needed to be exposed. This ultimately leads us to forgive our perpetrators and eventually learn to appreciate them for their harsh and painful lessons. Also, our life purpose requires us to shed the programming and conditioning of our genetics and childhood to go deeper within to find the true destiny of our lives. It is then our obligation to look at ourselves objectively outside of our egos, which are motivated by fear and not our heart's intelligence. The only way to purify gold is through fire. Diamonds start out as a lump of coal that withstands a tremendous amount of pressure over time. The only way to plant good crops is tirelessly till the soil. The only way to have knowledge of self is to go through hardships to expose our dysfunctions and false beliefs connected to unhealed traumas that need to be exposed to be corrected. Ancient Kemet metaphysics is the key to unlocking our freedom!

"When Israel was a child, I loved him, And out of Egypt I called My son."
-Hosea 11:1

CHAPTER TWO

XX Marks the Spot

In the beginning, in the ethers above the Earth, the Most High was contemplating and yearned to see It's reflection in this new low vibration, dense environment It just created called, the physical realm. The Most High split itself into two principles, one called the divine feminine, and the other principle called the divine masculine. The feminine principle represents the spiritual form of the Most High called, Woman and the masculine principle represent the physical form of the Most High called, Man. For the Most High to descend from the heavens to its lower vibration realm, It created a denser, heavier shell called the human form as its temple to house its feminine, spiritual aspect. Now the spiritual, feminine principle can embody itself in this physical form to experience itself in the lower vibrating, material realm. The feminine form of the Most High being magnetic, gathered all the materials in the Universe to make a Temple/Body to live in as it encapsulated itself. This was the "genesis" or (genes of the Kemetic goddess Isis) contribution to the human condition. The physical body represents the masculine principle and the spiritual body housed inside the physical body called the soul or spirit from the feminine principle. All from the One Creator! Once this being became too dense from the precious materials it gathered in the Universe, it fell from the ethers to the physical realm, coincidently losing its divinity in a slower, lower vibrating dimension filled with creatures programmed by fear and self-survival. The newly created human form forgot about its divine or feminine aspect housed in its body temple. The Most High was born a twin in this material world. One external twin it called man or male and the other internal twin represented by the woman or female. The Most High's main purpose on Earth was to have a sacred "reunion" with itself. In the hope of witnessing a divine reflection of itself in its partner to experience and appreciate the "Oneness" of its potential when its two divine, principles come together in balance and harmony in this lower-level dimension!

Before it came to the physical dimension, the feminine aspect of the Most High knew that it needed protection in this hostile, slow vibrating, low frequency environment. It assigned its masculine principle the sole duty and obligation of protecting and providing for Its spiritual, feminine self. It created the masculine principle bigger, faster and stronger than its feminine counterpart, which was vulnerable, compassionate, empathetic, nurturing, loving, healing and selfless. Thus, the masculine principle had to think fast on its feet and not be inhibited with emotion when it came to protecting It's twin feminine in high stressful situations. The masculine twin operated in logic first; emotions were delayed until the immediate threat was eliminated. It had to make quick decisions in times of attack and life and death situations. It had to be willing to sacrifice Itself for a divine being greater than Itself without thinking or having emotions about what must be done. This is the only reason the masculine twin was created. This was its sole purpose to protect It's spiritual, divine nature held in its feminine twin at all costs. This was Its only purpose in life and the sole purpose of Its creation. Over time, the male forgot about its divine duty to uphold and protect it's female twin counterpart and started to dominate, oppress and abuse her. He started to use his strength, his power and his logical mind that lacked empathy to manipulate her and treat her with scorn.

The feminine principle of the Most High is known by the XX chromosome. The masculine principle of the Most High is represented by the XY chromosome. The Y chromosome in the male principle is an exaggerated X chromosome of the female. For a male child to be born, the X chromosome gives permission for this to occur in the womb by manipulating one of her X chromosomes to becoming a Y chromosome. Thus, allowing a male child to be born in this dimension. The sacred feminine gives permission for the male child to be born. All life starts out as female. That's why men have nipples that don't serve any purpose. That's why we have a penis which is an exaggerated clitoris. Males have hanging testicles that used to be ovaries the fell outside the body. In this low vibrating dimension, over time, the Y chromosome in the male species develops an over exaggerated sense of Its physical self that metamorphizes into a false sense of identity known as the Ego. This concept was exclusively relegated to the male species has now infected the female species. Once this takes place, humanity is doomed to live its life without no concept of divine spirituality. The "Devil" now rules this dimension without humanity being the wiser. The "god" you worship is now the god of greed, fear, hate, cunning, deceit, gluttony, pride and shame. In antiquity, this personality trait has been given many names such as: Satan, Set, Zeus, demons, the devil, Lucifer, Shatan, Mark of the Beast, the Anti-Christ otherwise known as the Ego or Malignant Narcissism.

To further elaborate on this concept let's look at the timeless lessons of the Medu Neter and mythologies of ancient Kemet, particularly "The Ausarian Drama." The first god to resurrect himself was named Ausar he was depicted with the letter "X" on his chest, to represent the female principle otherwise known as the "X" chromosome. His wife, the goddess Auset, was depicted with a throne on top of her head, representing the concept of her mitochondria genes that are passed on from generation to generation through the mother. It was this matriarchal lineage or royal bloodline that the male was created to protect. The gene pool of the mother was the "throne" that the male species were made to protect, preserve, procreate and provide for. Her DNA was sacred. The story goes that Ausar was killed by his brother Set because he was jealous of him and his wife Auset. Set trapped Ausar in a sarcophagus, chopped him up into 14 pieces and scattered him across the land of Kemet. Auset's love and commitment was so strong for her husband, she searched far and wide gathering all his pieces to put him back together again. She found all his pieces except his penis, which was swallowed by a catfish in the river Nile. Once she put him back together again, she laid him on his back and straddled him. Once she did this, she turned into a bird and flapped her wings on top of him. She conceived a son that day and Ausar was resurrected in the afterlife where he sits on his throne and rules. The story goes that anybody who wants to go enter "heaven" must be escorted by his son Heru, who is seated at the right hand of his father, Ausar.

In this metaphysical story, Ausar represents the masculine principle. His brother Set, who killed him, represents Ausar's ego which always tries to supplant man's higher nature with his lower self. Auset represents Ausar's higher, spiritual nature contained in his feminine principle. She is the opposite of his lower self, represented by Set. Heru represents the consciousness Ausar, or the male species needs adopt to suppress their egos to resurrect themselves from the lower nature of their Y chromosome into their higher selves found in their X chromosome. Coincidently, Heru's name is where we get the word "hero" from. A hero is willing to sacrifice himself to save the damsel in distress. It takes the feminine principle represented by Auset to raise Ausar's consciousness by suppressing his ego represented by Set. This "kills" his lower nature so he can be resurrected into his higher self. This is why Ausar's resurrection is depicted as him wearing the "X" chromosome on his chest that symbolizes he has mastered his lower self, represented by the Y chromosome, by adopting the feminine principle located at his heart chakra. This is where the most powerful force in the universe resides. This awesome force is called Love, which Heru (the Hero in you,) represents. The concept of willing to die for a cause greater than yourself at the drop of a dime. This is what needs to take place for the divine union between a man and a woman to occur.

A peculiar thing happens when the Creator in human form incarnates into a physical realm. It loses all consciousness of its divine or sacred nature. During the birth process, humans experience multiple traumas which will affect their consciousness for the rest of Its's life. This divine, human form is ripped from the safety of its mother's womb as it comes into this new world headfirst. This creates a fear of abandonment as well as the fear of falling in the human subconscious mind. The divine being comes from complete darkness of the womb to suddenly enter an environment of extreme bright lights and loud noises. This creates a phobia in humans and develops a fear of sudden, loud bursts of noise and loud explosive sounds that emit bright colors that blind its vision. The divine being also comes from a very pleasurable environment of 98.6 degrees 24 hours a day, 7 days a week. Only to suddenly arrive in a cold, sterile environment of a chilling 68 degrees. This develops a trigger of shock when exposed to extreme temperatures as it matures into adulthood.

The Creator anticipated these harsh conditions, so it installed a cheat code inside of Itself to help it to remember who It is while It experiences this dense, harsh environment called the material world. That cheat code was there in the womb while it evolved and grew. That cheat code triggered the development and multiplication of Its cells while it comforted Itself with Its rhythm. That cheat code is the key to leading Its path back to the higher, unseen spiritual realm. That cheat code embodies the frequency we call Love to help guide It back to its original form after it has experienced Itself in this lower vibrating dimension. That cheat code is the Heart where the higher frequency of Love resides. XX marks the spot! We will get into the science of the heart and love later in the book.

Image of the god Ausar illustrating the letter X with his arms to symbolize his mastering of his animalistic Y chromosome which led to his initiation into the higher consciousness of the X chromosome of the female.

Secret Science of Sex

In the occult, the symbol of the upside-down triangle represents the feminine principle. She is represented by coming down from heavens. Whereas the symbol of the masculine principle is represented by the upright triangle rising from the earth. God gathered the earth's minerals and nutrients from the soil and made them denser. This creates a triangle from the base to a denser point at the top. That's why in the story of Adam in the Bible; he is created from the earth or the soil. But Eve or the feminine principle in antiquity always comes from the heavens. Eve or the feminine principle starts off as a less dense frequency in the spiritual realm then is made dense by accumulating the materials needed as they come to a point. This heaviness allows her to fall from the heavens to Earth to meet the male principle that was already here. The male principle vibrates at a lower, slower rate that is why it is bound to the Earth. The female principle vibrates at a higher, faster frequency. Thus, the woman represents spiritual nature of man, and the male represents man's lower physical nature. These principles come together to bond in harmony here on Earth. The upright triangle represents the male being masculine. Masculine is always portrayed by the plus sign, a positive or a plus. Positive just means to post or to sit still because man at his optimal level needs to have a strong foundation to create and release his optimal energy. He must have a strong foundation to be able to give off the best in him. If his foundation is suspect and weak, his energy is going to be unstable and not sustainable. If he has a strong foundation based on integrity, character, morals, values and principles, then his energy will be that much more powerful and fruitful. The masculine principle is represented by the plus or positive sign. The horizontal line is the testicles and the vertical line below the testicles or horizontal line represents the male phallus at the rested state. The phallus is ready to give off energy at its heightened erect state represented by the vertical line above the horizontal line. These intersecting lines represent the male phallus at its rested and ready to give off energy states. Positive energy is labeled as masculine energy. It means to post or sit still. It gives off energy and does not receive it. That's its simple definition. European doctrine has labeled the word "positive" as something good or correct because it's attached to the male principle. Masculinity is the foundation of their entire culture and system of white supremacy. It is based on white male domination of the world. It can be defined as having no spiritual conceptions, no compassion or empathy towards others. Everything is not personal, it's just business. The concept of the survival of the fittest has its genesis in the masculine principle. It is the embodiment of masculinity. This is the white male's worldview and diabolical nature. On the contrary, we have the female principle represented by the upside-down triangle. She's represented by the negative sign displayed by a line going horizontally. We know that the female organ is designed as a vertical slit, but they turned it sideways in this representation to confuse you. The negative principle doesn't mean the feminine principle is bad. The word negative literally means to "have no gates." The female principle has no boundaries. She's an infinite being. She is spiritual by nature. The feminine principle "receives energy" as opposed to giving out energy like the masculine principle. The feminine principle is stronger because it is not limited to the laws of physics of the material world. Which one is the stronger principle, the one that can give a punch or the one that can take a punch? The feminine principle is the stronger one that can take a punch and keep going.

This sign is called the Star of David, the Sephedet, the Seal of Solomon, Anahata and the Tetrahedron. It represents the sacred union of the male principle and female principle coming together in balance and harmony. This creates a sacred union. Inside the sacred union, is the divine hexagon shape. This shape is the "Gateway" from the spiritual realm that leads to the physical realm. One can manifest from the spiritual world to the physical realm, i.e. have a child. But it doesn't stop there. Ideas can be manifested. Health issues, anything you want from your thoughts can enter this physical dimension through access of this "Gateway!" Also, the opposite can be true. When we transition or die the heart opens to create this gateway to higher spiritual dimensions. It's known as the Anahata located in the Heart chakra. From the physical dimension our spirits can escape gravity through the higher frequency and the gateway of the heart. Gravity represents the "grave to the soul" as our souls are trapped inside the prison of the physical body. Once we reach higher, spiritual consciousness or the vibratory frequency of the heart, which is 528 hertz, we gain enough velocity to escape "grave-ity" so we can travel to higher spiritual dimensions the Bible refers to as Heaven. If we don't reach the frequency of 528 hertz held in the heart chakra, at the time of our transition, our souls will be reincarnated back into this physical realm to repeat our life sentence for eternity.

Instead of Black people creating a sacred union based on balance, harmony and love, we have created a Scared Cohesion coming together in a trauma bond. It's based on the generational, dysfunctional conditioning and programming of our inner child abuses and wounds. There's a mutual understanding amongst Black people in the relationship of accepting each other's dysfunctions and insecurities by lying to each other and not addressing real issues to heal childhood wounds. This dysfunctional cohesion based on trauma, becomes the standard of our relationships. This is not a sacred union. It is a generational scar that is passed on as normalcy. These relationships are based on lower-level emotions. This is where the cohesion comes into play. Cohesion can be defined as "the action or fact of forming a united whole. The water-soluble part of the relationship is the female, and the oil-based part of the relationship is the male. In their natural state they separate and are not cohesive, as they are opposites. But when you agitate them by creating drama and stress, there is an illusion of cohesion. The shaking up of the bottle is traumatic. It is the lower-level activity that fuels the relationship. It is the arguments, the breakup to makeup, the jealousy, the rage, the physical and mental abuse. This is what's holding the relationship together artificially. These Scarred Cohesion relationships need to be shaken up constantly to produce artificial cohesion. Without the drama, these two elements of water (female) and oil (male) separate naturally when there is no disturbance. We need to get back to the Sacred Union and not settle for Scarred Cohesion.

What does a Sacred Union look like on an anatomical or molecular level? Let's look at the first element on the Periodical Table. That element is Hydrogen which is the basic building block that all the other elements use as its foundation. The hydrogen atom consists of one proton which is the male principle that represents the man. It gives off energy because that's what men do. Men post up and sit still to give off energy to attract a female electron who receives that energy and decides that she is getting all her needs met and chooses to stick around. The electron or female will revolve around the proton or man. The man gives out his energy to the woman. The female electron is attracted to that energy and decides to revolve around the man and multiples the man's energy and reflects it back to him creating the circumference of their reality. Without the woman, or electron, the man, or proton would never know his potential or how great he can become. The woman is the motivation and mirror to the man's potential. If he attracts a bad mirror, female, because he is giving off bad energy, he will see himself as such and the woman reflect a dysfunctional relationship back to him. If the man is of good standing and giving off good energy, then that female will give off the reflection of the best in him and inspire him to achieve higher heights.

The space in between the proton and electron is the potential world they can create together. Once they combine as one in a Sacred Union, they create another element outside of themselves. Contrary to popular belief, the man must lose himself in the union and the woman must lose herself in the union to create a new element that has its own properties. The man doesn't fully lose all of himself because he's still and always will be the proton represented by masculinity. The woman doesn't completely lose herself because she's always the standard of the feminine aspect of nature, represented by the Electron. They create in the circumference of their reality a new element. Is the element good? Is it bad? That's for that relationship to decide that depends on the consciousness of the new creation. This happens on a molecular level on every cell in your body trillions and trillions of times. This is the standard of nature and the way God created relationships to begin with. Men having strong foundations based on integrity, character, giving off that energy and the female finding that energy attractive, taking that energy, multiplying it, and giving it back to the man to create the circumference of their reality.

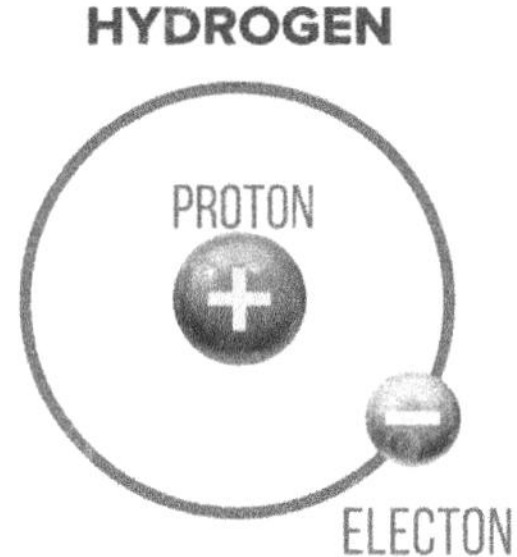

We can also see this very symbolism in the Hindu religion. In the image you have the female deity Shakti representing the feminine principle (-), sitting on the lap of the male deity named Shiva, representing the masculine principle (+). Shakti represents the female electron atom. Shiva is the male principle, represented by, the black figure in the image, is the proton. Notice Shiva sits still and Shakti revolves around him.to create the circumference of their reality based on the Sacred Union. This position is called the Yab Yum which is like the Yin and Yang image.

Yab-yum (Tibetan literally, "father-mother") is a common symbol in the Buddhist art of India, Bhutan, Nepal, and Tibet. It represents the primordial union of wisdom and compassion, depicted as a male deity in sexual union with his female consort. The male figure represents compassion and skillful means, while the female partner represents insight.

Ying Yang infographic template. Two in one. yin and Yang symbol of dualism in ancient Chinese philosophy where opposite or contrary forces are complementary yin and Yang symbol of dualism in ancient Chinese philosophy where opposite or contrary forces are complementary. Like light and dark or fire and water, male and female.

In ancient Kemet, you have the original Trinity. You have male god Ausar. He represents the proton. He's located in the middle of the other two deities just like the proton in the Hydrogen molecule. He's giving off his energy. He is the masculine principle, the male personified, the proton (+). The female god Auset represents the electron atom. She is on Ausar's left-hand side. She receives the masculine energy from Ausar as she revolves around him and reflects his masculine energy back to him. This creates their Sacred Union. In their union they naturally create a neutron atom or a masculine centered deity by the name of Heru. This is why their god son is a male. Neutron atoms hang out with masculine protons. He's the divine product of the Sacred Union. The Golden Child. The word hero comes from the god Heru. When a man and woman come together in balance and harmony at the level of the heart, they create a Sacred Union. The byproduct of this union produces a Superhero!

The original Holy Trinity from ancient Kemet. It consists of the god Ausar, in the middle exalting the X chromosome, on is left is his wife, the goddess Auset and their son the god Heru who sits at the right hand of his father. All principles are accounted for in one sacred union of balance and harmony.

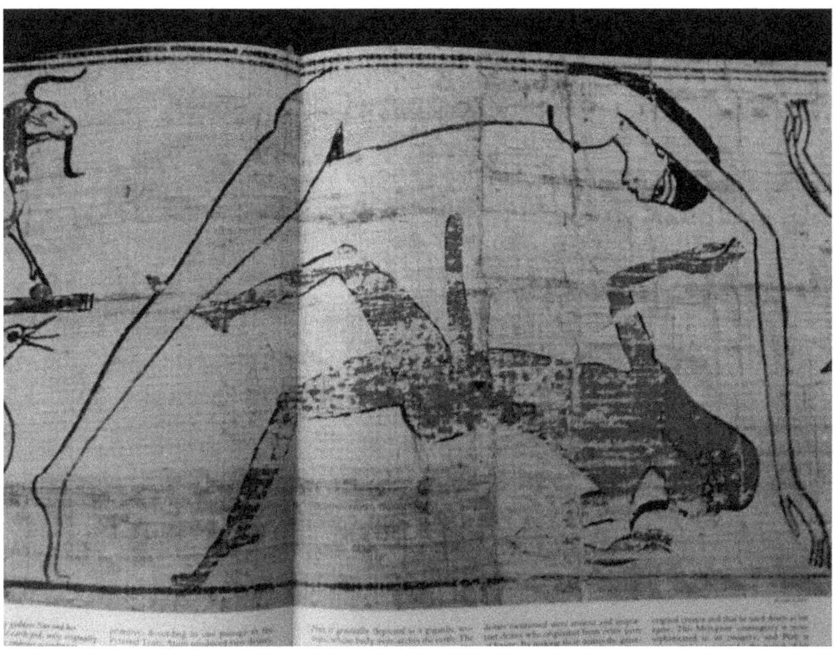

Image of the goddess Nut (the sky goddess), the god Geb, her brother (the god of the earth) & the god Shu (the atmosphere between the two) in ancient Kemet representing the sacred union found in the basic building block of the physical dimension called the Hydrogen atom.

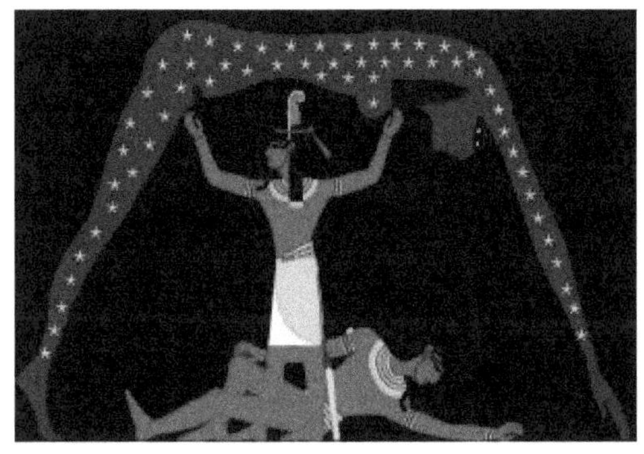

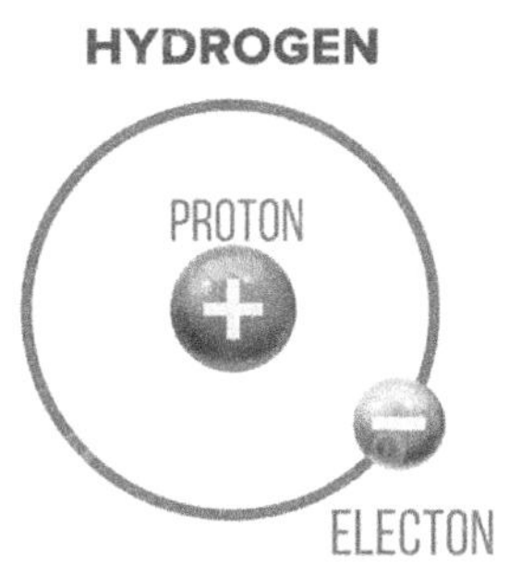

This space between the sibling deities of Nut and Geb is called the goddess Shu. The Sky god Nut is the feminine principle or electron atom (-). Her brother Geb representing the Earth is the masculine principle or the proton (+). Just like the Biblical Adam, the deity Geb comes from the earth. Geb sits still as his sister Nut representing the sky, revolves around him as the stars seem to revolve around the Earth. This is another representation of the Sacred Union. Masculine and feminine principles come together in balance and harmony at the level of the heart. This phenomenon creates the goddess, Shu. Shu is their divine creation that creates the circumference of the two deities' reality. Shu represents the empty space of possibilities between two atoms that is filled by the level of consciousness shared by the two deities coming together. These two-dimensional images I provided are really 3D pictorial representations of subatomic occurrences that are constantly in motion in the unseen or spiritual realm.

Consequently, in the Ifa religious tradition, the goddess Oshun has very similar qualities to the Kemetic goddess Shu. Not only do their names sound the same, but they are both represented by the colors green and gold. Green represents the heart chakra, and gold is the illumination of the heart which is where love can be found. Oshun is the goddess of love also represented by the honeybee. Bees create honey in hexagonal honeycombs. This hexagonal shape is the same sacred geometry as the tetrahedron, or the Anahata Merkabah held in the heart chakra. Remember, the heart chakra resonates at 528 htz. which is the frequency of love. The goddess Oshun and the goddess Shu represent the frequency of love. In the middle of the feminine and masculine principles coming together in balance and harmony produces the frequency of love. The goddess Oshun or Shu creates the atmosphere of this Sacred Union. This is where we get the word Atmosphere or to be more specific, "Adam's Sphere." This is the "circumference of their reality" of this Sacred Union. The proton, represented by the Biblical Adam, sits still on his strong foundation and gives out energy. The electron or Eve is sustained by Adam's energy and starts to evolve around Adam. Eve creates the circumference of their reality otherwise known as "Adam's Sphere" or the word Atmosphere. This is the level of consciousness this couple will operate from in their ability to manifest their reality. This is also why the goddess Oshun is always holding up a hand mirror to see her reflection. It is not out of vanity, it is metaphysical. Oshun, who represents the female electron, is the reflection of the masculine proton.

The goddess Oshun in the Ifa tradition symbolizing Love, who I connected to the Kemetic god Shu in the Kemetic tradition. Love fills the space of the atom to create a sacred union between man and a woman.

Metaphysics of the Divine Union

My understanding of the metaphysics of relationships is based on the Periodical Table, Ancient Vedic mythology and Kemetic Universal Laws & Principles, which were the most advanced civilization known to man. Why not study the culture where man excelled at its highest level to interpret reality and set the tone for the things we need today to resurrect ourselves to a higher level of consciousness?

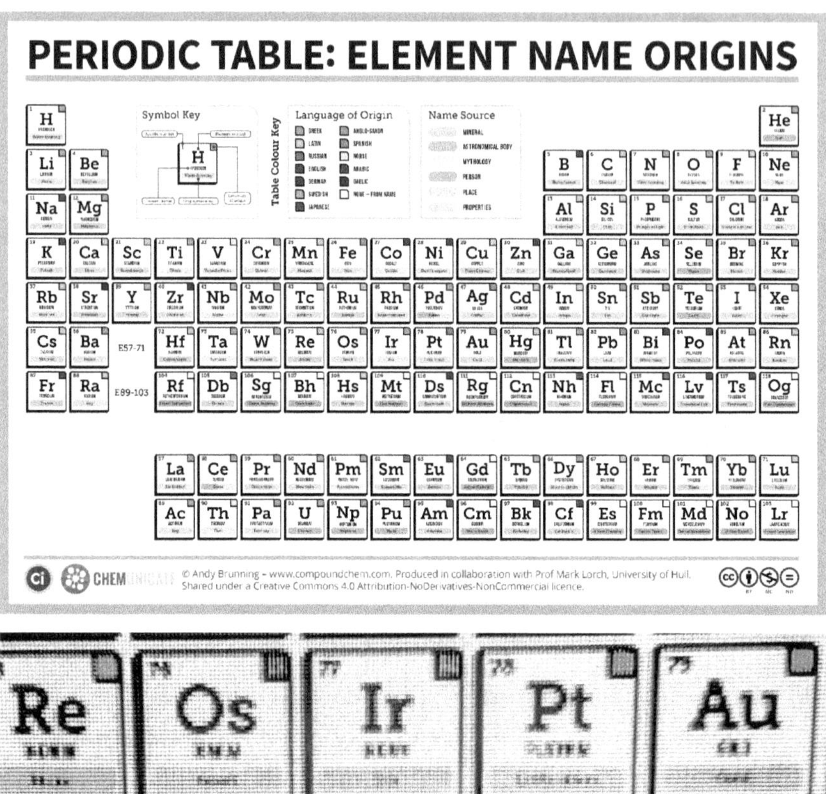

On the Periodical Table, the Kemetic gods Re or Ra, Os-Ir(is), PT(ah) and AU(set) are all represented.

CHAPTER THREE

Trauma Bond

Ancient, Kemetic people referred to themselves as gods and goddesses walking on Earth. It wasn't an ego trip of I'm God and everyone's lower than me or I'm a goddess and everyone needs to bow down to me. It was more of a symbol of trying to reach perfection through generations after generations implementing a culture to help raise the collective consciousness so that they can be as close to God as possible. It was a journey. It was a mindset of the perpetual pursuit of the mind, the body and the spirit at its highest level. This procedure was started with arranged marriages. Arranged marriages get a bad rap today but there was a method to this ancient custom. They took their most elite, son and matched him with the elite daughter of another royal family. Their parents were on a quest to perfect themselves so any parental idiosyncrasies, traumas, abuses, or character flaws that the parents had before conception, they made sure that they took care of them in their lifetime, so they didn't pass on generational curses and dysfunctions to their children. You can imagine if every mother and father here in America overcame their obesity and addictions. Overcame their childhood traumas. Overcame their impoverished mentality and their abandonment issues. Overcame their daddy and mommy issues. Overcame their egos, fears and triggers and then created an offspring that didn't have to deal with those traumas. They did this generation after generation where the goal was to create a god here on Earth not an egotistical God but a child as close to a spiritual being you can become. There was a cultural program that transcended generations, made to uplift the best in humankind and suppress the ego. Man was not an animal having a human experience, but a divine, spiritual being trapped in a physical body. We are all made of imperfect material, but we should strive to be perfect. We should strive to turn that imperfect material into perfection as much as we can. This science is known as Alchemy. We can never come close to reaching perfection, but the goal of society back then was to create a divine child and that starts with working on yourself before you even try to produce an offspring. They also looked up at the stars to guide them in their procreation. Astrology, as it's called today or the Horoscope, meaning the Kemetic god Horus, which is the Hero and Scope, meaning the eyes to see the hero in you and how to activate the hero in you even before you came into existence. It was divinely planned. You were an enlightened Indigo child that was planned years ago before you were conceived. There's a verse in the Bible that says, "In my house there are many mansions." It refers to the 12 zodiac signs that coincide with the month, year and time. These signs have houses or compartments within the sign that tells you about your personality. Tells you about your insecurities. Tells you about what makes you successful, what makes you happy. What makes you sad. It is a blueprint to your life contained in these houses. The ancients understood if you look to the stars, they could guide you with your spiritual life purpose. "As Above So Below." The same thing as you see down here on Earth is a reflection held in the night sky. It was a mirror to Earth. When you looked up you were looking at yourself. But you had to have the code to decipher the celestial bodies. We're not going to get too deep into astrology as it can get intense, but I want you to know that there's things that we can use today to help us pick a mate, to help us create a" golden child." To help further our genetic material by purifying it instead of passing on our childhood traumas, abuses, fears and dysfunctional idiosyncrasies to our children for them to deal with. "In my father's house there are many mansions." There are 12 Zodiac signs. I was born a Scorpio in November. I'm a "fixed" sign. All 12 zodiac signs have three foundations or personality types within that sign. Within the sign, if you were born in the beginning of that sign, you were a Cardinal sign. If you were born in the middle of the sign you were a Fixed sign. If you were born towards the end of your zodiac sign you were a Mutable sign. These months fluctuate as zodiac signs go from one month to another. To recap, you have the Cardinal sign which is born in the earlier days of that zodiac sign. You have the Fixed sign, which you were born in the middle of that zodiac sign, and you have the Mutable sign, which is being born at the end of that zodiac sign. Being a Cardinal sign means your personality type brings energy to whatever you participate in. You are the initiator. The party doesn't start until you get there. You get things popping. You get things going. If you are a Fixed sign like I am, you are the foundation of that zodiac sign. You are unwavering in your disposition. You represent the energy of that zodiac sign's personality trait represents. You are accountable. You are a rock and represent stability and consistency. Then you have the Mutable sign. You were born on the last days of your zodiac sign period. You represent the closer. You are the finisher and get things done. You make sure everything is all wrapped up in a bow with no loose ends.

When you are picking someone to be your mate it's very vital that you study their astrological chart. Ask yourself, "what type of personality do they have and does is complement yours?" If you are both starters, it may not work out. You may clash naturally. If you are both finishers, you may have disharmony as one may not want to let go of the reins. If you are both Fixed signs, there can only be one foundation, and your partner may not want to budge. Simple things may be serious issues if left unrecognized.

People talk usually only talk about their Sun sign, but you also have a Moon sign. You also have a Rising sign. These signs also reveal a person's personality trait. The Sun sign, mine being Scorpio, is your ego's interpretation of who you will be in the Physical Realm. My Moon sign is in Taurus. Your moon sign is your spiritual representation or your spiritual interpretation of you how you define yourself in this physical reality. It's your "higher self." Whereas your Sun sign is your" lower self." To truly know a person, you need to know their Moon sign. The moon only comes out at night so that represents the hidden or unseen spiritual aspect of your personality. You have your Rising sign. My Rising sign is Leo. Your Rising sign is the personality trait that you need to adopt to find your purpose in this life. Me being a Scorpio, I rather live under my rock. I am a loner by nature. I value my privacy. I don't like the spotlight or want to be the center of attention. I don't need an audience to motivate me. I am a self-starter. When you lift my rock and expose or disturb me, that's when you feel my stinger. But if you leave me alone and let me do my thing, I am very peaceful, benevolent and content. I let my work speak for itself. My Moon sign which happens to be Taurus is the exact opposite of my Scorpio Sun sign. I have a good balance of physical and spiritual awareness. I'm a good marriage to myself. Taurus is grounded. Everything I do is based on foundation and stability. I don't get too high or get too low. I stay balanced but when you mess with a bull you get the horns! Bulls are very loyal but Scorpios are very individualistic so there is a battle there. To be able to find my purpose I must look to my Rising sign, which is Leo. To maintain my purpose, I must be the lion not the Scorpio. I must come up from under that rock and get out of my comfort zone. I must be seen and I have to be heard. I must be in the forefront no longer invisible in the back. I must overcome my shyness, my insecurities and fears. It does me disservice because no one can experience the gifts that I have to give to the world. I must push myself out of my comfort zone constantly. I must be the lion and roar and let people know that I'm here. That I'm powerful and I am strong. I have something of value that can help others.

Those are the three signs that I would like you to look up for yourself. Look up the time, date and the place you were born. That will tell you your birth chart and you can find out the three signs you fall under as well as all the houses that make up your personality traits and who would be the best mate for you. Each zodiac sign is represented by an element. There are four elements, that means there's three signs per element. I am a water sign Scorpio along with Cancer and Pisces. The characteristics of water are as flows; very adaptable, water goes with the flow, very self-sufficient, cohesive and magnetic. Water has the capacity to transcend to a higher form. Water is the source of life. Water purifies and cleanses. Water never dies it just changes forms. If water meets a frigid energy, it will become impenetrable, stern and hard. If water meets a heated energy it will want to escape. Water cannot be contained for long periods of time; it will find its way out. Water searches for the lowest common denominator and will attempt to raise it. These are the concepts of water signs found in Cancer, Scorpio, and Pisces. This is just another aspect of your personality as it goes deeper than just that. There are several houses. These are just guidelines of a foundation on how to fully have knowledge of self to give you the best chance to succeed in life and find a mate that holds you accountable by complementing you.

Air signs are Gemini Libra and Aquarius. The properties of air. Air wants to be free it does not want to be contained. Air will always want to escape containment, or it will become stagnant and deflated. Air wants to express itself freely. When under pressure, air gets stronger. Air is very adaptable in any environment. When agitated, air rises to the top and expands. Air is very adaptable when it gets cold, it gets depressed and sinks to the bottom. Air wants to be in the background or behind the scenes. It lets its work speak for itself. Air is strong willed and even tempered but can be destructive. It is uplifting when it is supported.

Taurus, Virgo and Capricorn are the Earth signs. These signs are always grounded, down to earth even keeled and levelheaded. They are practical, safe and consistent. Their highs are not too high and lows are not too low. They are stable, reliable, accountable and steadfast. They normally are in control and slow to anger. But when pushed to the limit they will explode on you! The whole world shakes at the point of no return. The last set of signs fall under the element of fire. What are the characteristics of fire? Fire wants to burn and be free. It cannot be contained. Fire wants to express itself freely. Fire does not apologize because it feels no need to. You either get it or you don't. Fire can be very destructive depending on who is using it. It can also bring life and healing. Fire is a self-starter but others can feed it or starve it. Fire's behavior can be misunderstood sometimes. Fire can give you new life but only after it destroys you. Fire wants to express itself it wants to be heard and when it's not heard there's a storm ready to happen. The best way to deal with fire is to let it express itself in a controlled environment and give it enough oxygen, meaning individual attention.

Each zodiac sign is attached to a part of the body. They also correspond to a particular number and color. Each zodiac sign is either feminine or masculine which has little do to with being a man or woman. When choosing a mate there's a lot that should go in it and not just the feeling they give you. We need to go back and look at how our ancient ancestors, who were the most advanced civilization in the history of the world chose their partner to procreate with it. It was science. It was deliberate rite you had the responsibility for your generational DNA to advance to divinity. You did that by choosing a partner that would help elevate the best in you and suppress the worst in you. For example, Aries rules the head body part and its color is red and it's number is one. On the other hand, Taurus rules the neck and throat body parts and its color is indigo. It also resonates with the number two. The zodiac sign, Gemini the rules arms, hands and shoulders. Its color is yellow and it resonates with the number three. The zodiac sign Cancer, rules the stomach, resonates with the color green and light green and the number is four. The zodiac sign, Leo rules the back and spine and resonates the color is orange. It's number is five. The zodiac sign Virgo rules a nervous system and intestines; its color is violet and resonates with the number seven. The zodiac sign, Scorpio rules the sexual organs, resonates with the color burgundy or maroon. It resonates with the number eight. The zodiac sign Sagittarius rules the hips and thighs its resonates with the color purple. Its number is nine. The zodiac sign Capricorn rules the knees it resonates with the color green and the number ten. The zodiac sign Aquarius rules the shins and ankles and resonates with the color is light blue and the number eleven. The zodiac sign Pisces rules the feet and resonates with the color turquoise and the number twelve. There is a science for numbers called numerology. I will list a basic image of the main numbers you need to interpret.

Basically, the **number one (1)** represents Unity. It represents self-sufficiency and the best in you. You need nothing outside of yourself to acquire your life purpose and your heart's desires.

The **number two** (2) represents separation or division. There's something that we need to separate or divide from to achieve our life's purpose. We need to objectively look at ourselves in the mirror.

The **number three** (3) represents Divine Perfection of the mother the feminine the father the masculine to create the child. It is the best in you. The balance of masculine and feminine energy to create the best version of yourself.

The **number four** (4) represents the four corners of creation in this Matrix. To create and manifest here you need the balance and harmony of the physical, emotional, spiritual and intellectual self. This creates the third dimension.

The number five (5) represents God's grace. You are covered knowing that if you do wrong the Most High knows your heart and all Is forgiven. If you can forgive yourself, you stay in his grace.

The **number six (6)** represents man as an animal having a human experience only interested in food clothing shelter Transportation avoiding pain and seeking pleasure

The **number seven (7)** represents divine completion. There are seven days of the week. There are seven keys on the piano. Seven layers of skin. There are seven chakras. It's the number of divine completion. The way to obtaining higher levels of consciousness is being initiated by completing ascending cycles.

The **number eight (8)** represents eternity or Infinity. It represents doing the same thing repeatedly and thinking you're going to get a different result. This is the very definition of insanity. You must be willing to get out of your own way to reach higher levels of consciousness. If you turn the number eight sideways you get the infinity sign.

The **number nine (9)** is the number six which represents man as an animal turned upside down. What is the lesson that you need to learn to move your consciousness forward? Your life is being turned upside down to see what deficiencies you need to address. Man's true character is not shown when things are going right but when they are seemingly going wrong. That's when you find out what you are truly about.

The **number ten (10)** is the number one, the divine in you, standing next to 360 degrees of knowledge which equals perfection. Being able to tap into the "God in you!"

The **number eleven (11)** is one more than perfection. You're looking in the mirror to see what you are about and show who you are by seeing your reflection. Your flaws will be exposed, or you will like what you see.

The **number twelve (12)** is the number of completion. 12 months in a year. 12 jurors in a jury. 12 grades in primary school. 12 apostles who followed Jesus. Must complete a cycle to move forward in your consciousness.

The **number thirteen (13)** is the number of resurrection. Twelve jurors and the thirteenth is the judge. Twelve months and the thirteenth month is the new year. Twelve disciples and the thirteenth one is Jesus. It is the number of rebirth, transformation, resurrection, new beginnings and new life.

We talked about the color frequencies as they related to each zodiac sign. Let's look at the chakra system to determine what these colors represent on a metaphysical level. Here's a quick overview. The Chakra colors of red, orange and yellow represent the element of fire or man living in Hell. The person's consciousness is operating at a lower-level state of self-survival. This person is only interested in obtaining food, shelter, clothing, transportation, avoiding pain and seeking pleasure. This is all they are conscious of. They go to the job they hate, paying bills, going to the club, smoking weed and playing video games or going shopping. They do the same thing repeatedly. They go to church every week, but their morals and values never change. They try diet after diet and get gym membership after membership but never better themselves physically. They haven't broken past their fear of lack and self-survival. That's why Hell is considered eternal because you keep doing the same thing repeatedly thinking you're going to get a different result. Which is the very definition of insanity. The color with red, orange and yellow hues symbolize man as a beast or animal. The lowest level of consciousness man can descend to. The green colored hues represent the heart. The heart is the first level of higher consciousness of man. The heart is where love exclusively resides. Where love is unconditional. Where man is willing to die for others and a cause greater than itself. Where humans have compassion, empathy and are selfless. They are humble, nurturing and healing. The blue colored hues represent communication. The best form of communication is listening while you sit still. This is the best form of hustling as it brings clarity to your journey. You are in tune of your surroundings. You have knowledge of self and a heightened state of intuition. You have discernment as you open your first eye so that you can see beyond the illusion. The purple-colored hues identify humans as spiritual beings having a human experience.

If you're picking a mate know these things about yourself, your potential mate. Pass on the information to your partner so they can consciously work on the things that keep them in a lower state of consciousness. Study how the parts of the body assigned to each zodiac sign may be a precursor to a spiritual imbalance and not just a physical ailment. Harmony equals hormones in balance. Disease means dis-ease or imbalance in the body. From the feet to the knees to the sexual organs on up, everything in your body is related to your zodiac signs. This is where you will see stress first. That's where you're going to see the imbalance

As a people, we need to go back and reclaim our science. This is why they demonized the Horoscope or Zodiac science and made it frivolous. This is why they said it was devil worship and went against God. They don't want you to create a god. They want you to stay at a lower level of state of consciousness and never reach your full potential. You're easily manipulated and controlled by fear in your present state. You are a child who is very easily manipulated. You have not overcome your addictions. You have not been healed from your traumas and childhood abuses. They keep you locked in there as; Western medicine does not cure it treats disease. It treats the side effects so that you can continue to be sick for a longer period. It doesn't cure you or address the spiritual nature of disease. They don't want you to unlock the greatness that lies in your DNA that your ancestors passed down to you. You have the blueprint on how to create gods and goddesses here on Earth. Divine children are never conceived and given birth to. Only an amalgamation of broken, dysfunctional spirits that inherited unresolved abuses, addictions and traumas from their parents. You can never see divinity in yourself because your science has been taken away. Now you fear looking up at the stars. You fear looking up at your reflection because someone told you it's the devil. But in truth, it's the face of the Most High. You!

"Women need to heal so the little girl inside of them can come out. Men need to heal the hurt little boy in them so that the man can arrive." – TC Carrier

Let's address the LGBTIQQ community and what attracts them to each other to build a dysfunctional community. What is the attraction that motivated these people to build a strong and politically powerful community and are very influential economically and now have a voice and a seat at the table when it comes to so-called civil rights and discrimination. They are galvanized and now are inclusive when it comes to political power and obtaining resources for their cause. One thing that I realized when confiding with people in this community is over 90% have experienced some type of sexual abuse or trauma as children. They do not acknowledge that a common "prerequisite" for being involved in this community is having suffered traumatic abuses as a child and mainly of the sexual nature.

When the child is experiencing sexual trauma in real time, they will compartmentalize the trauma as a way of protecting their sanity and innocence. As a defense mechanism a child will protect their innocence from the overload of this heinous act. It is very traumatic both physically, emotionally, mentally and spiritually. The moment sexual abuse occurs they check out of their bodies and mentally file the experience deep into the recesses of their brain to isolate, separate and neutralize the experience while they are in the process of going through it.

The sexual trauma will remain here under lock and key and will never be opened and addressed even as they become adults. It's just too traumatic and too painful to deal with the first time so going back in revisiting it is not an option. The sexual trauma as a child, now gives you the okay as an adult to open that box in the recesses of your mind not to heal and address it but to actually participate in the sexual activity that you were forced to as an innocent child. Your community will justify this sexual behavior and say you are normal when in reality you are acting out a childhood trauma that you never fully addressed or healed from. Your are then justified acting out this behavior by given the excuse that you were born this way and nothing needs to be addressed or is dysfunctional about this behavior. The community tells you, you did not decide to be this way, and you didn't have any choice in this matter. The acceptance of this behavior and the unconditional support from your community now locks you into a lifetime of pain, shame and the inability to address the root of the problem so that one can finally heal and be whole. Now one lives their life justifying their lifestyle, which is nothing more than a reaction to sexual trauma they were brutally exposed to as an innocent child.

This causes a chain reaction in the community, and the cycle of broken, unhealed people continues. There is no pride in not addressing and healing from your sexual trauma as a child.

Now these two victims come together bringing their childhood sexual trauma into their relationship and now you have two like-minded or like experiences as children that understand one another's pain. They have empathy from one another. They want to love each other to heal but they don't know what healthy physical displays of affection look like. Their first sexual experience was being raped. They get together because of the trauma bond union and act out their sexual trauma as children against each other and sadly call it love. Their community supports and encourages this dysfunctional relationship while they suffer and don't understand why they still can't obtain happiness. This community is known for their promiscuity. You have a group of unhealed, hurt people searching for love outside of themselves not realizing they will never find it until they heal their inner child who suffers in silence inside of them. Their inner child was forgotten and is still locked in the recesses of their psyche still waiting for the adult you to come back and get them and tell them it is safe to come outside.

Is it common knowledge that any abuse one suffers as a child you will more than likely abuse someone more vulnerable than you in the same manner if you do not heal. Psychology tells us that the person who was abused wants to get some semblance of their power that was taken away from them, so they perpetuate the abuse on others. Now they can experience the power of the perpetrator, but it doesn't last so they seek more victims and call it searching for love. But the so-called, "Love" never arrives just more pain, shame and depression.

As a sexually abused child you quickly realize if you don't fight or resist the rape, you can find some semblance of pleasure in the trauma as a way of coping with it. The more you fight, the more pain you feel. They are conditioned to having sexual trauma be pleasurable for them. Over time their Predator is grooming them and telling them that they love them. Tell them that they're special. Tell them that they have a secret that only they can share because you are special to them. They love you so much you start to ingrain that in your mind and now the abuse is misinterpreted as love. You've been trained and you've been groomed. Now you're susceptible to it and you allow yourself to start feeling pleasure again as a way of escaping. You question yourself because now sexual abuse is pleasurable to you. It is the, "If you can't beat them, join them." mentality. As you grow into adulthood you become almost guilty of feeling and wanting pleasure. You feel that you were the one that wanted the abuse in the first place, not knowing your innocence was taken away from you without your consent even if you remained compliant and silent. It wasn't uncle, coach, babysitter, cousin or aunt, mother or father, who's 30 years older than you. Who's stronger than you. Who was manipulative and played mind tricks on an 8-year-old and their minimal understanding of the world. Now the ideology of love is exchanged for guilty pleasure. Not realizing they only experienced pleasure because they allowed themselves to think that their predator loved them. Thay they were special to them. It opened these fears and insecurities and self-doubt and they started believing in. Now they're older and feel guilty subconsciously of what they did because they did receive some level of pleasure from it to escape. They forget that they were at an impressionable age where their body and mind were still developing. For you to be put through such a traumatic abusive experience by someone you love, and you trusted that's a lot to deal with

It's not your fault. It never was your fault. You were a victim and your innocence was taken advantage of by a person who was a monster and was willing to take the innocence of a child knowing that they would never be the same again. For their own personal fleeting satisfaction. I always relate this type of behavior to picking the fruit off a tree before it has a chance to ripen. Once that fruit is taken off the branch, the fruit will never mature. You can't put the fruit back on to the branch of the tree so that it can fully develop. It stuns its growth and will always remain green no matter how long time passes. If you never address the trauma, you will never attain the best version of yourself. I hope you find peace and love and healing so that we can all move forward in our self-actualization and not be stuck in a trauma bond that's now accepted as being normal

THE FACE OF GOD

Is there such a thing as Pretty Privilege? Do beautiful people have an easier life? Do they get things for free? Do people make an easier way for them wherever they go? The answer is yes. And let me tell you why. And it's not what you think it is. In ancient Kemet, there was no separation between the word God and the word nature. Nature meant God. And God was nature. They looked in nature for the divine and they found the "Face of God." Our ancestors found a particular pattern that was hidden in plain sight throughout all life forms, throughout nature. It was a sequence of fractions and angles that seemed to multiply at a certain rate. Later, they called it the Fibonacci sequence, also the Golden Ratio. This is what is meant when the Bible says, "to see God in all things." You are literally seeing the blueprint of life or the divine or sacredness of all life which starts with the Fibonacci Sequence or the Golden Ratio. They duplicated this pattern in all their temples and statues. This is how you saw "God." It was a sequence. It was a ratio. They found out when man looked at this ratio, he didn't know exactly what he was seeing but he was seeing the face of God or the divinity in man. This is what makes person beautiful without us knowing why.

This is what makes them attractive. It's your subconscious mind understanding that you're literally seeing God's blueprint in the person that you are looking at. This is the standard of beauty. It's the Golden Ratio. It's the Fibonacci sequence in you. That is the divine. You are seeing the face of God in human form. This is why attractive people have an easier life. People want to give things to them. They want to do things for them. They want to go out their way to make sure that they're comfortable, that they're taken care of. It's because subconsciously they are seeing the face of the divine. This is why men get on their knees and bow down when they want the woman of their dreams. In the observer's sub-conscious mind they're seeing the face of God and they're giving reverence to that. This is also why when men mess up in a relationship, they get on their knees and beg for the woman to stay with them again. They know that they are seeing the divine and must show humility to keep them. This is also why chivalry is not dead. Men still know subconsciously that they are in care and custody of the divine being. So yes, attractive people do have an advantage, but now it's up to that person not to abuse this divine power that they were given. If you use these powers to stunt or to promote ego and self-worship, then you are doing a disservice to the creator. But if you humble yourself and show compassion and nurturing and honor and integrity and character and humility, then you are honoring the character of the creator. If you are using your attractiveness to promote lower-level deeds, lower-level thoughts and actions, then you are working for the devil. The Bible warns us of this behavior in Matthew 7:15. It warns us against false prophets who pair harmless on the outside but are inwardly destructive. In the King James version, the verse says, "Beware of false prophets which come to you in sheep's clothing, but inwardly they are ravaging wolves." You see, attractive people have a responsibility to their creator to uplift humanity and not to lower humanity and to the ego and animalistic desires and passions. Yes, attractive people have a higher standard that they must uplift to for they were given the gift, the gift of the divine, not egotistical self-worship and self-aggrandizing. This is what you call classic beauty. Inside and out having character and integrity. What are you doing with your attractiveness? Do you raise people consciousness to be a better human being? Are you a prime example of a leader with morals and values and integrity? Or do you glorify the ego and exploitation? Attractiveness comes in all packages. And I guess we're all mixed between our higher and lower selves. and how we use our attractiveness. But understand in the system of white supremacy, Black attractiveness is used to be exploited and to promote the worst in us. So, for those attractive people, the choice is yours. Are you exploiting your attractiveness for personal gain and riches and money by selling your soul? Or are you living with humility, integrity, morals, and values and uplifting your people to higher heights? The choice has always been yours but understand you are held to a higher standard.

CHAPTER FOUR
We Make Hell Comfortable

Before we can plot a course as to what we want to become in the future, we must not only have knowledge of self but also know where we are at in the present moment. It has come to my knowledge from years of soul searching, research and experiencing life's difficult lessons, that this physical dimension and the system we are subjected to, is the place the Bible refers to as Hell. Remember, everything that yearns to survive in this physical world must kill and consume another living being to do so. From the plant kingdom to the animal kingdom to bacteria and parasites, every creature is forced to be a serial killer to survive. We live in a world that forces all life to participate in the murder of innocent life in one form or another. This is what we eloquently describe as the "Circle of Life." This is a low vibration realm that nourishes and rewards the animalistic nature in all creatures and promotes fear. I also believe that this lower-level consciousness is cyclical as all things in this realm are on a time cycle. We just happen to be in an Age where Lucifer reigns and people that emulate his consciousness rule the world currently. I believe the Age where our ancestors ruled the world was a Golden Age of higher consciousness, spiritual awareness and metaphysical marvels! That time will come again but for now we all choose to be here at this time in this place. I believe a select few of us are the Initiators and spiritual warriors that came to help humanity transcend into a new consciousness as we usher in a new Age of Aquarius, which is the Age of "I Know." We are exiting the Age of Pisces or the Age of "I Believe." Humanity is waking up from the consciousness of "Believing" to the higher consciousness of "Knowing!"

"How art thou have fallen from heaven, O Lucifer, son of the morning! How art thou cut down to the ground which didst weakened the nations."-Isaiah 14: 12 KJV

Let us investigate the etymology of the name Lucifer which the Bible refers to as the "Anti-Christ. Lucifer literally means the "bearer of light." He was God's favorite angel. He is the leader of the so-called "fallen angels" who were cast out of heaven into Hell because he rebelled against God. The name Lucifer refers to his former splendor as the greatest of all the angels and God's favorite!

Let us metaphysically breakdown this Bible scripture and the definition of Lucifer and see what can be decoded from it. The scripture states that Lucifer, "fell or was cast out" from heaven. As we know everything in the Universe is energy which cannot be created nor destroyed. This means that energy is constant in its existence. It is timeless. Energy can be separated and categorized by its frequency and vibration. Each frequency has a specific characteristic unique to itself, like cell phones have a unique frequency that can be communicated with by your specific cell phone number. That number or frequency is exclusive to you or whoever is assigned that sequence of numbers. Frequencies are often defined by two characteristics, high frequency and low frequency. Higher frequencies have shorter wave lengths and lower frequencies have longer wave lengths. If we use this fact as a foundation in deciphering this Bible verse it is basically saying "Heaven" is a realm of higher frequency and Lucifer was "cast out and fell" to a lower frequency of existence. The Bible, also mentions Lucifer is in control of all the

"Fallen Angels." We can deduct that Lucifer was not the only entity/ energy to "fall" from a higher frequency, known as "Heaven," to a lower frequency known as "Hell." Lucifer is also in charge of all the lower-level frequencies, known as demons or devils who reside in Hell.

Let us decipher what are the major differences of higher and lower frequencies besides their bandwidths? The higher the frequency the faster the velocity of the energy which makes it less dense and hard or impossible to detect with our five senses although it exists all around us. It is invisible to our naked eye. And our other senses cannot detect it. The lower the frequency means the slower the velocity of the energy which makes it denser. The material world is made up of the same energy as the spiritual dimension, but since it is of lower, slower frequency it has the "illusion" of being solid, liquid or gas. This allows our five senses to observe it; thus, it creates the physical dimension from which we define ourselves and our environment. In a nutshell "higher frequency" can be called "Heaven," which is ruled by God and cannot be detected by our five senses and lower frequency can be called "Hell," ruled by Lucifer, which is the material or physical world.

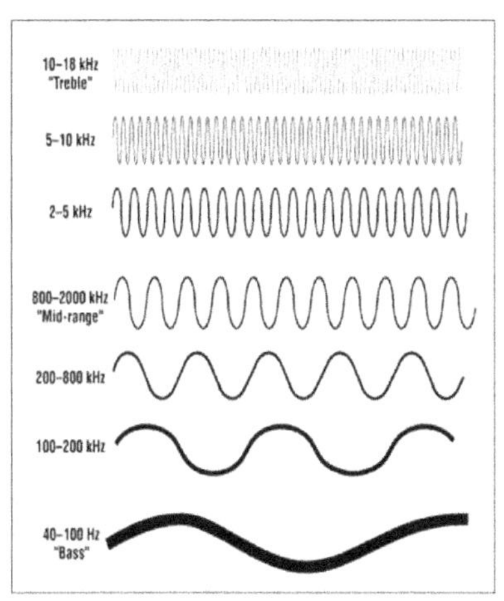

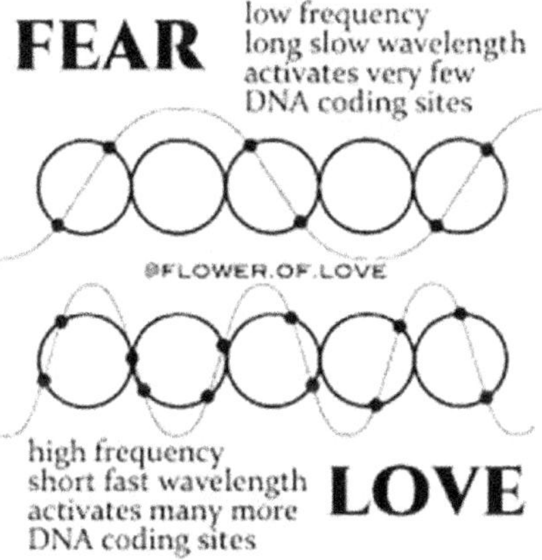

In the image above, one sees different frequencies represented by their wave lengths. The lower frequencies at the bottom of the image have long, looping wavelengths which make them slower and denser, which creates the material world. The higher frequencies on top of the image have faster, shorter wavelengths. This causes them to be less dense and impossible for our five senses to detect.

Lucifer literally means the "bearer of light." If Lucifer is associated with light that means in "Heaven," Lucifer was a high frequency of light. When he rebelled against God, his frequency dropped and automatically "fell" to a lower frequency or as the Bible puts it, "was cast out" of Heaven. We can conclude that low frequency light is the physical dimension. If Lucifer is low frequency light and now embodies the physical dimension, we can deduct that the physical dimension is Hell which the fallen angel named, Lucifer rules with his other "fallen angels" or should I say, "fallen or descending Angles of low frequency light." The physical dimension is made up of photons. Photons are particles of light. The physical dimension is made of "solid" matter. Solid matter is really particles of light or atoms moving at a slower vibration to give the illusion of having characteristics of being solid. It is photons or particles of light, which I refer to as Faux-tons or light "Faking" to be solid." Faux is a French word for false or fake. Atoms are composed of a dense nucleus, enveloped by a cloud of electrons whirling at tremendous speeds. The nucleus, home to protons and neutrons, makes up an incredibly small fraction of the atom's volume, while the vast area between the nucleus and its electron cloud remains empty. The distance between the nucleus and the electrons is analogous to a pea in the center of a football stadium, with the electrons akin to tiny flies buzzing around the outermost seats. This atomic arrangement leads to the conclusion that atoms—and thus matter—are mostly vast empty space!

This lower frequency of light that creates this dimension, is Lucifer, the Light Bearer's creation! That's why there is a popular saying amongst Christians, "The devil promises you everything but gives you nothing." This dimension from which we identify ourselves and our environment as "physical" is nothing more than **"F.alse E.vidence A.ppearing R.eal."**

(FEAR.) It is particles of light moving at a slower rate, which creates the illusion of matter. Because of the programming and manipulation of our five senses by Lucifer, which are our only means of detecting this realm, we have been conditioned to accept it as our reality without question. Thus, it becomes real and absolute, undisputed truth and fact. This is what the movie The Matrix was pointing out. You are living in a simulation that keeps you in a state of constant fear to keep you asleep and unconscious.

"And the great dragon was cast out, that old serpent, called the Devil, and Satan, which deceive the whole world: he was cast out into the earth, and his angels were cast out with him."
-Revelation 12:9

Words that describe Lucifer or the Devil.

- Lucifer **"Fell" from or was "kicked out"** of heaven. **(Dropped to a lower frequency.)** This suggests that at one time Lucifer was operating at a higher level of consciousness referred to as "Heaven." Then he starts to define himself through his Ego or his lower self, which lowers his level of consciousness and he "falls" down to the physical dimension that has a slower, lower vibration. The material world is made up of slower and lower vibrations. Earth now becomes Lucifer's dominion to rule over unsuspecting humankind.
- Lucifer was the **most beautiful angel in heaven**. **(Law of Attraction.)** God testifies that out of all his angels, Lucifer was the most beautiful, enlightened, talented & attractive. He even admits that Lucifer was His favorite out of all the angels! One of Lucifer's greatest assets and weapons is his ability to attract, deceive, manipulate and seduce humans to worship and participate in his lower-level frequency activities. "The Devil promises you the world

but gives you nothing and takes everything." This is why social media and advertisements are so prevalent and persuasive. There is no substance, it is a lie or falsehood. It's all about perception and appearance but it is just an illusion. This is the culture of Lucifer. "Fake it to you make it," mentality. But never internalize the sacrifices you need to experience self-actualization to become something of substance based on humility, integrity, character, selflessness and compassion.

- Lucifer **created and controlled the most beautiful, angelic music in heaven! (Master of Frequency.)** This is another clue about the powers Lucifer possesses. The fact that Lucifer oversaw all the music in heaven means he was a master of sound, vibration and frequency. It is this character trait that suggests that Lucifer's greatest skill set, his greatest weapon, is his manipulation of sound, light, music and language/anguish in this realm. The basic building block of the physical dimension is sound, frequency and vibration. Also, the power of the tongue is a powerful weapon and creates spells! This is where the power lies in this domain! You are in the realm of Lucifer. You are in Hell. You have just made Hell comfortable when you should be trying to escape it you embrace it.
- Lucifer was **God's favorite angel. (Dichotomy of man.)** The fact that Lucifer was God's favorite angel suggests that he had the potential to be righteous but chose to rebel. All humans have the free will to decide which "God" they will serve. You can serve your higher, spiritual self or lower your frequency and serve the ego. The Bible makes it clear no one can serve two masters. You are either following your heart as a spiritual being having a human experience or you are in your ego motivated by fear, greed, shame and the selfishness of a beast. The greatest gift the Creator gave the human race is the free will to choose who they will follow and embody! Lucifer has tricked you into thinking you are worshipping the best in you, but you are actually serving him without you

even knowing it! Now he gives you the illusion of choice as he manipulates every decision you make on a daily basis.

"So, because you are lukewarm-neither hot nor cold-I am about to spit you out of my mouth."
- Revelation 3:16

- Scripture calls Satan the: **"Prince of the power of the air, the spirit who now works in the sons of disobedience," - Ephesians 2:2**

"The Air" referring to the power of **sound, vibration, frequency, and in particular music, words & language** (anguish) that oppresses humanity. They all travel undetected through the air waves manipulating your behavior without you knowing it.

- Lucifer getting **"kicked out"** of heaven (the unseen realm or spiritual dimension) to rule **"Hell"** or the **physical dimension scientist call the "Light Spectrum,"** as all matter is made of light or photons/(fake) **fauxtons.**
- Lucifer means **"The Light Bearer."** It is no coincidence that the secret societies that rule the world are called **"The Illuminati,"** which means the illuminated ones, or the ones who can see in the dark or through the illusion of light, which I believe is, **The Electro-Magnetic Light Spectrum or Hell**. These secret societies know where they are and help Lucifer in secrecy to keep his rule and dominion over humanity.

The last two examples above, I introduced the concept of the electromagnetic or light spectrum. Let's dig deeper into this concept and how it relates to: Lucifer the "Light Bearer," language, sound & frequency and the "Illuminated Ones" otherwise known as the Illuminati. Below is a diagram of the Electromagnetic Light Spectrum, also known as, the Light Spectrum. It is this miniscule sliver of energy that looks like a rainbow, contained in the electromagnetic spectrum that is visible to humans. All other energies in the image below in black, we cannot detect with our five senses.

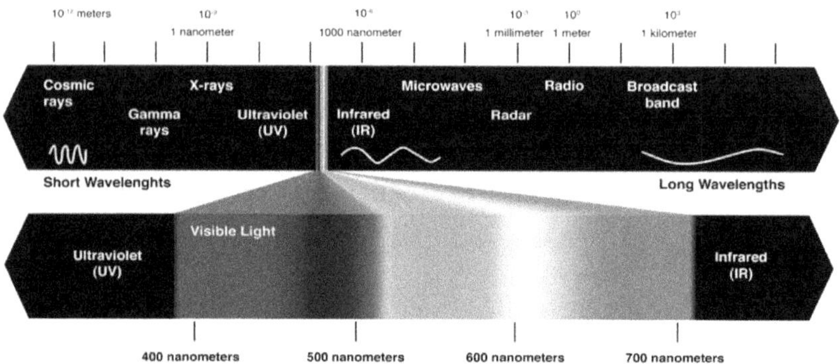

You can observe above, in between Ultraviolet (UV) light and Infrared (IR) light, is a small, rainbow slither of what is called Visible Light. It is made up of 7 major colors or frequencies, otherwise referred to as the Chakras in Eastern spiritual philosophy or the Rainbow. It consists of the vibrational waves of Red, Orange, Yellow, Green, Blue, Indigo & Purple in that order. Each color or frequency holds a unique characteristic that is attached to the human condition and emotion (Energy in Motion.) This minuscule portion of energy is the only section of visible light that we as humans can detect with our five senses. That means there is over 99 % of light or energy that we cannot detect with our five senses. We are literally going through life as human beings in complete darkness and blind to the majority of energy that is contained in our physical world. The Fallen Angels, instructed by Lucifer, exploit this human deficiency to manipulate, oppress and subjugate us under their rule in a ruthless attempt to literally keep us deaf, dumb and blind while we serve their agenda at the expense of our own sovereignty. Coincidently, the Fallen Angels feed our egos or man as an animal, since before birth to motivate us by fear and fear alone. Fear is the most powerful motivator and controller of human behavior. Because fear is the absence of love, without love there is no hope. There is no healing.

There is no compassion nor empathy. Thus, there is no escaping, Hell. When you can manipulate human emotions, you can predict how a human will respond to any given environment that you expose them to. The people become his slaves without one chain or whip being used. The best slave is the one slave that doesn't realize he is being enslaved. Lucifer works in the unseen light or boundaries of the light spectrum. This is where he whispers in your ear and where we get the phrase, "The devil made me do it!" We are all groomed to be addicts in one form or another. You just don't know you are an addict. Because addicts are easily manipulated and controlled by their addictions, Lucifer has laid out for you to consume like a buffet. Welcome to Hell if nobody told or greeted you!

"And no marvel; for Satan himself is transformed into an angel of light." -2 Corinthians 11:14

Let us further break down this realm we occupy based on lower-level frequencies of light and expose how we can navigate through it to find our life's purpose and eventually escape Hell. How did Lucifer create this realm and how does it function at such a high level of deception to have enslaved billions of lost souls? Answer, he created a diabolical prison with cells for your soul that have no bars or walls, that you voluntarily take with you wherever you go.

Question, what object separates light? Answer: A prism. A prism or "prison" traps white light and redirects its angles "angels" to separate it into seven main colors we call the electro-magnetic light spectrum. Lucifer's seven "Fallen Angels/Angles" manipulate humans from the unseen realm. These seven colors or fallen angles, coincide with the seven chakras that originated in Kemet and mentioned in the Veda text of ancient spiritual knowledge.

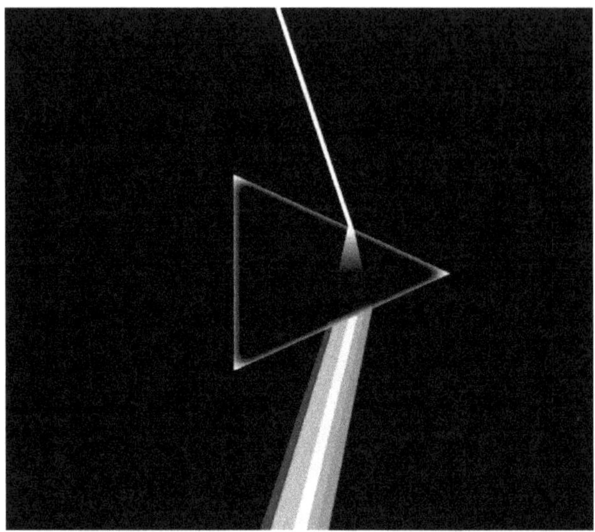

The image above is a pyramid or Prism/Prison separating the "Fallen Angels or Falling Angles of Light" otherwise known as Lucifer's fallen angels. He created the Electro-Magnetic Light Spectrum, that produces the Chakra system from which human emotions (Energy in Motion) are secretly manipulated in the so-called illusion of the physical realm he created.

The seven chakra energy centers in your body align from the base of the human spine to the top of the human head. Each chakra represents a level of consciousness the human condition can descend or ascend to. The first chakra is the root chakra which is red in color. This energy center represents man as an animal only interested in food, shelter, clothing, transportation, avoiding pain and seeking pleasure. This is where 90% of humans dwell. Working in jobs they may not like for the majority of their lives only interested in paying their bills to obtain the things that I aforementioned. The second level of consciousness is held in the Sacral chakra located at the sexual organs, which is the color orange. It represents man's consciousness only being interested and motivated by the things that give him pleasure. He has no moral compass to guide him and only creates and does things for his own selfish pursuit to pleasure and please himself. He will avoid painful and uncomfortable situations that are outside of his comfort zone at all costs, even to his own detriment. The third chakra is located in the solar plexus and is represented by the color yellow. This center of consciousness holds your passions, desires and addictions. It is the unadulterated fire that burns inside of you. It is only interested in the pursuit of those said things without a moral compass or integrity to guide it. This will always lead to lower-level behaviors, interpretations and definitions of your reality. These first three chakras are known as man's "Lower Self." This consciousness can be defined as man as an animal only motivated by satisfying his carnal needs and wants. This is the "beast" in man that the Bible refers to by the number 666 that we all have the potential to define ourselves and our reality by. It represents 6 Protons, 6 Electrons and 6 Neutrons which is the atomic structure of the element, Carbon. Carbon is the basic building block of our physical, human bodies which trap our souls in this dimension. Or man defining himself as an animal. It is our egos that cannot look at itself objectively, justifies our devious behaviors and addictions, always a victim and never takes accountability or self-sacrifices for others. It is also these three chakras or lower-level frequencies in man that Lucifer manipulates and controls us with. It is no coincidence that these three chakras are the same colors as the element fire: red, orange and yellow. The Bible describes a place called Hell as fire, brimstone, gnashing of teeth (stress) and eternal suffering. This can be translated as being stuck in a consciousness of self-survival, me first, no discipline, no morals, addicted to sex, porn, money, gambling, alcohol, food, weed, social media, gym, church, work and justifying your behavior by never forgiving and being a perpetual victim. Also, the Bible describes Hell as "the gnashing of teeth." This description relates to the stress this behavioral lifestyle comes with. We grind our teeth and clinch our jaws when we are in a perpetual state of stress. Even in our sleep! This is a sign of hypertension or high blood pressure, which is referred to as the "Silent Killer." Lucifer is a silent Assassin!

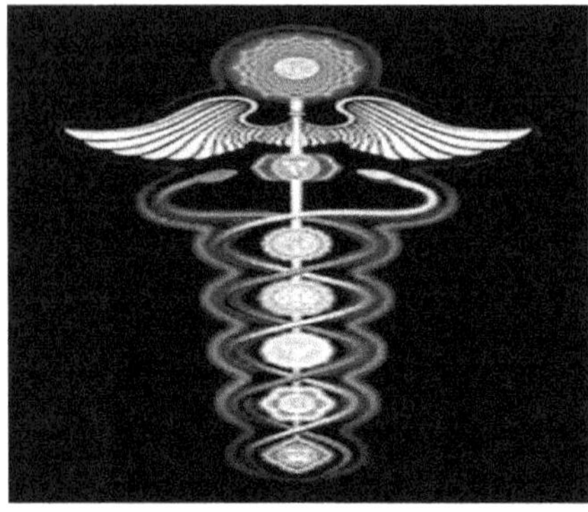

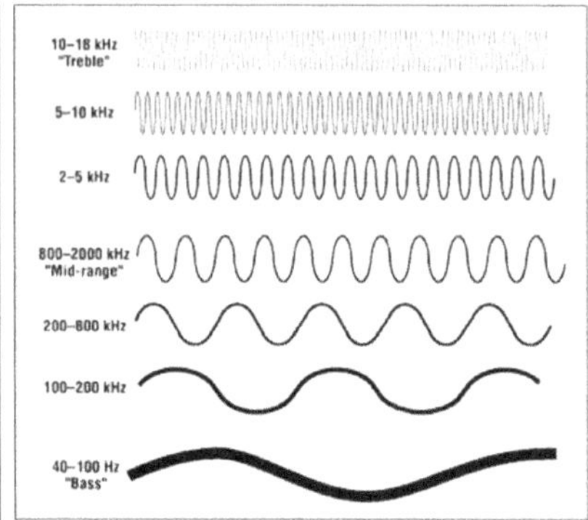

The seven chakras system described by ancient Veda texts coinciding with their matching frequencies in the middle image. Notice the Caduceus in the image on the left you see the wings on top of the staff to symbolize "escaping/transcending" this lower frequency dimension!

How do we escape this physical dimension that the "Light Bearer" rules otherwise known as Hell? Our ancient, melanated ancestors left clues all around us, waiting for the day we would raise our frequencies and finally decipher them. That day has arrived! These clues were strategically left around the world at different sacred ley line sites or energy centers of the Earth. They etched them on gigantic, megalithic stone structures that can stand the test of time, waiting for us to awaken one day to be able to translate them and follow their instructions. That time is now in the Age of Aquarius. Aquarius' motto or frequency is, "To Know." It is no coincidence that on top of the entrance way to the temples in Kemet read the inscription. "Know Thyself." The Age of Aquarius is represented by the woman bearing a gourd of water ready to wash away all the falsehoods and illusions of its predecessor, the Age of Pisces, which is the Age of "I Believe." We do not believe blindly anymore. The Age of the fish being led by "schools" without independent thought is behind us now. We are not being "hooked" by shiny things with no substance. We see the "bait" and are no longer attracted to it. We are not motivated by fear of staying in groups that choose indoctrination and acceptance over truth.

It has been revealed that gravity defies all logic and principles of why and how it exists remains a mystery. It is one of the biggest misnomers in nature yet to be unlocked. The root word of Gravity is Grave. If Lucifer is the ruler of this lower frequency realm made from low frequency light, then he uses the force of gravity to keep our souls trapped in hell for eternity. Hell is the grave to the soul. How does one spirit overcome the grave or gravity? Simple, become lighter than the opposing force that keeps you here. How does one soul become lighter than gravity? The ancient Kemetic goddess Maat tells us that our hearts need to be as "light as a feather" to enter the kingdom of heaven. How can we make our hearts as light as a feather? Simple, the goddess instructs us through her 42 negative confessions or laws that we are supposed to repeat daily after our day concludes. Coincidently, this is where we get the ten commandments from. A summary of the laws can be simplified into: Suppress the Ego, Forgive others & yourself, Show humility, Have Integrity, Don't participate in falsehood, celebrate truth, Overcome fears & traumas, Show compassion, Empathy, Practice selflessness, Feed the hungry, Clothe the naked, Do not be deceitful, Sacrifice for others & be willing to die for a cause greater than yourself. Interesting how these aspects of "lightening your heart" sound vaguely familiar to describe the characters; Jesus, Moses, Buddha, Shiva, Allah, Kwan Yin, Oshun, Heru and every other religious iconic deity that has defied death through resurrection? In fact, don't Christians say Jesus lives in their hearts? Don't they show the image of the heart with a flame coming out the top of it with a crown of thorns around it to symbolize the new life Jesus has for you if you follow him? This is not to be taken literally as literal translation of the Bible is the lowest level of consciousness to decipher its meanings. We are not kindergarteners anymore. We have graduated to higher levels of innerstanding! Once you have achieved this higher frequency located at the level of the heart or Love, that is faster than the opposing velocity of gravity known as the "grave for the soul," one may escape or rise above this dimension and may now enter the "kingdom of heaven." Let the church say, "Amen!"

The Sacred Heart of Jesus on the left. Notice the light or one's soul "escaping Hell" from the illuminated heart! On the right, is The Weighing of the heart ceremony with the goddess Maat to enter Heaven. Your heart must be as "light as a feather!"

It is no wonder that the first level of higher consciousness is found in the heart chakra, which is green. The heart chakra is the place where healing takes place in pure love with no fear. It embodies forgiveness, compassion, empathy, nurturing, selflessness, humility and self-sacrifice. To escape the three lower-level chakras, you need to embody the heart chakra's consciousness. This is also why Hell is considered eternal. This lower-level consciousness cannot get out of its own way. It keeps doing the same things repeatedly thinking it will get a different result. This as you know is the definition of insanity. Hell is an insane asylum. The embracing of the heart's consciousness is the hack to get out of Hell. Now you are operating in your "higher self" which can be defined as a spiritual being having a human experience. This is how your spirit escapes the Prism/Prison of light. This is how you unlock the "cells" in your body that incarcerate your soul upon your incarnation.

Florence Baptisry mural, created c.1260, by Coppo di Marcovaldo

Most fast-food restaurants use the colors of specific chakra energy levels to manipulate its customers into purchasing their food. The color red or Root Chakra communicates to your primal, animalistic characteristics, such as hunger and self-survival and the color yellow or Solar Plexus Chakra, communicates with your primordial desires, addictions, and passions. Using these two specific color combinations in their logos, manipulate unsuspecting individuals who see these signs, into acting according to their animalistic hunger, desires, addictions and immediate self-gratification without rational thought or discernment.

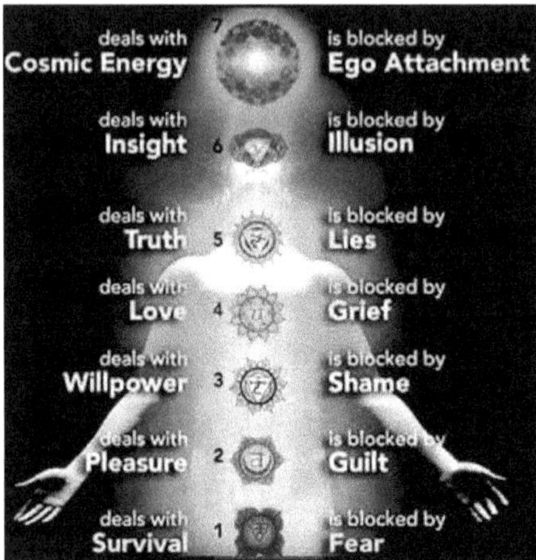

Color	Wavelength
violet	380–450 nm
blue	450–495 nm
green	495–570 nm
yellow	570–590 nm
orange	590–620 nm
red	620–750 nm

Most fast-food restaurants use the colors of specific chakra energy levels to manipulate its customers into purchasing their food. The color red or Root Chakra communicates to your primal, animalistic characteristics, such as hunger and self-survival and the color yellow or Solar Plexus Chakra, communicates with your primordial desires, addictions, and passions. Using these two specific color combinations in their logos, manipulate unsuspecting individuals who see these signs, into acting according to their animalistic hunger, desires, addictions and immediate self-gratification without rational thought or discernment.

The seven chakras in the middle image above. The first 3 represent your lower self with the fourth chakra being the heart. The first chakra to higher consciousness. On the right is a chart recognizing each frequency matched to a given chakra. Each wavelength matches a certain human level of consciousness or emotion otherwise known as, "Energy In Motion." Image on the left, The Heart Chakra, the first level of higher consciousness & the "Gateway" to heaven!

CHAPTER FIVE

Prism Planet

What is humanity's fascination of the rainbow, which represents the Electro-Magnetic Light Spectrum Lucifer manipulates to create the illusion of our "so-called" physical reality.

Mythology of the Rainbow

- In Greek mythology, the goddess Iris was the goddess of rainbows. Iris is also the part of the eye that allows us to see. Her job was to send messages from the gods to man concerning warfare and retribution. She also would carry water from the river Styx to the gods. The river Styx runs through a place called Hades, otherwise known as Hell. Does Lucifer manipulate the "Iris" in our eyes to deceive us to do his bidding in this dimension?
- In West Africa, among the Benin people they worshipped the rainbow god, Ayida-Weddo is known as the "Rainbow Serpent." In the Bible, Satan is also depicted as a snake.
- For the Karen people of Burma, the rainbow is considered as a painted and dangerous demon that eats children.
- In Māori mythology there are several personifications for the rainbow, depending on its form, who usually appear representing

omens and are appealed to during times of war. The most widespread of these are Uenuku and Kahukura.

- In Chinese mythology, Hong is a two-headed dragon that represents the rainbow. The rainbow being associated with the serpent also represented Lucifer in the Bible.
- In Mesoamerican culture, Ix Chel is a maternal jaguar goddess associated with rain. Chel means rainbow in the Yucatán Poqomchi' language. Ix Chel wears a serpent headdress.
- Many Aboriginal Australian mythologies include a Rainbow Serpent deity, the name and characteristics of which vary according to cultural traditions. It is often seen as a creator god, and as a force of destruction.
- The Sumu of Honduras and Nicaragua refer to the rainbow as walasa aniwe, "the devil is vexed". These people hide their children in their huts to keep them from looking or pointing at the rainbow.
- In Amazonian cultures, rainbows have long been associated with malign spirits that cause harm, such as miscarriages and (especially) skin problems. In the Amuesha language of central Peru, certain diseases are called ayona'achartan, meaning "the rainbow hurt my skin". A tradition of closing one's mouth at the sight of a rainbow in order to avoid disease appears to pre-date the Incan empire.
- In Ireland, a common legend asserts that a pot of gold is to be found at the end of a rainbow, guarded by a leprechaun, who is a trickster, mischievous and can't be trusted.
- In the Hebrew Book of Genesis, after the flood had almost wiped out the entire human race, God told Noah that he will set the rainbow as a token of his promise that he would never send another flood large enough to destroy all life. The rainbow appearing after death and destruction.

- The rainbow is depicted as an archer's bow in Hindu mythology. Indra, the god of thunder and war, uses the rainbow to shoot arrows of lightning.
- The Sumerian farmer god Ninurta defended Sumer with a bow and arrow, and wore a crown described as a rainbow.
- According to syncretic Malay shamanism and folklore, the rainbow is said to have been formed from the sword of the earth serpent Sakatimuna who was defeated by the archangel Gabriel.
- In Bulgarian legends, it is said that a person who walk beneath a rainbow will change genders: a man will begin to think like a woman, and a woman will begin to think like a man. This is interesting as the LBGTQ community has adopted the rainbow as its moniker.
- The Fang of Gabon, Africa, also prohibit their children from looking at the rainbow.
- In the mythology of ancient Slavs, a man touched by the rainbow is drawn to heaven and becomes a "Planetnik" – half-demonic creature – which is under the power of the thunder and lightning god Perun.
- The first movie in color came out in 1939 it was, "The Wizard of Oz." It also contained the most popular song ever recorded about a rainbow entitled, "Somewhere Under the Rainbow." This is significant in our breaking down of the realm which humans reside in. The movie takes place in middle America, in the state of Kansas. Kansas represents the middle of America or the heartland or "heart chakra" of America. "America's Heartland." The state of Kansas is also shaped as a square whose sides total 360 degrees of "hidden" knowledge in the Occult. Lucifer with the help of the entertainment industry, wants to hit the "Heart" of America to instill its science and knowledge to manipulate and control the masses for eternity.

"Over the Rainbow" is a classic ballad song with music by Harold Arlen and lyrics by Yip Harburg. It was written for the 1939 film The Wizard of Oz and performed by actress Judy Garland in her starring role as Dorothy Gale. The song is one of Garland's most iconic performances and has since been covered by numerous artists in many different styles.

Over the Rainbow

Song by Judy Garland

Somewhere over the rainbow, way up high
There's a land that I heard of once in a lullaby
Somewhere over the rainbow, skies are blue
And the dreams that you dare to dream really do come true
Someday I'll wish upon a star
And wake up where the clouds are far behind me
Where troubles melt like lemon drops
Away above the chimney tops
That's where you'll find me
Somewhere over the rainbow, bluebirds fly
Birds fly over the rainbow
Why, then, oh, why can't I?
Somewhere over the rainbow, bluebirds fly
Birds fly over the rainbow
Why, then, oh, why can't I?
If happy little bluebirds fly
Beyond the rainbow
Why, oh, why can't I?

---Source: LyricFind. Songwriters: Harold Arlen / Yip Harburg

This song has resonated with many people around the world and has become a beloved classic because it captures a universal feeling of longing for a better world and the hopeful belief that such a place exists somewhere. It's a testament to the power of dreams and the human capacity for hope knowing there so much more than what meets the eye. Tragically, Judy Garland led a tortured life after she played this role and eventually succumbed to her many addictions. I believe playing this role led to her demise as she couldn't be seen successful in life as she was onscreen and must be shown trapped in the system that oppressed her. She may have escaped the system in the movie, but they enslaved her in real life. Coincidently, Hollywood is known for discrediting stars in real life for characters they portrayed in a good light on the big screen. For example, Jim Caviezel who played Jesus Christ in the blockbuster film, "The Passion of the Christ," his next role he played a deranged serial killer. Monica Belluci who played his mother Mary in that same movie, was brutally raped in another feature film she starred in after this role.

Let us break down this historic movie which set the tone for how Hollywood does Lucifer's dirty work by being a major tool to suppress, influence and manipulate the masses without them even knowing it.

- The movie starts off in black and white. "The Wizard of Oz" was the first movie to be used in color! The beginning of the movie in black and white signifies that Dorothy has no knowledge of herself or the world she lives in. She is a slave and doesn't even know it. Thus, her worldview is limited to the two basic colors of black and white with no "gray areas" or knowledge in the unseen or spiritual realm.
- When Dorothy is transported to the Land of Oz she immediately sees things in vibrant colors and illumination! This symbolizes Dorothy's initiation into higher consciousness. She is now waking up to the knowledge of self and her environment and is discovering that the world she used to live in was really her dream and this new world was her reality!

- Dorothy's only companion through this shift in consciousness was her fateful, Black dog named Toto. Toto represents the ancient Egyptian god named, Anpu or his Greek name, Anubis. Anpu represents our intuition that dwells in our higher self. He represents our 6th chakra known as our "First Eye." He guides us in the spiritual realm. The world outside of the light spectrum that we can't, see, touch, taste, hear or smell. For us to utilize our intuitive, higher state we must raise our consciousness and follow our hearts and not be fooled by what seems illogical in the physical realm.
- This is why Dorothy must "follow the yellow brick road" to find her true self and get back "home" represents her higher self. The road made of gold bricks is Dorothy overcoming her fears and lower self to stay on the path her heart has laid out for her. It is the road from your lower self that leads to your heart. The "Gateway" to higher consciousness to escape "Hell."
- The road is treacherous at times and very scary, but Dorothy stays steadfast, overcomes her fears and stays the course. This is what every individual must do to meet their "true" or higher, spiritual self.

The first character Dorothy meets on her journey to find her higher self is the Scare Crow. In legal terms, on all legal documents your name is in all capital letters. This name is called your Straw Man. It is on your driver's license, passport, car note, mortgage, court and legal documents and credit cards. Your "Straw Man" represents you as a volunteer slave to a system that thinks of you in terms of your earning power and potential to make money off you over your lifetime. You are bonded to a lifetime of slavery and don't even know it. From the time they issue you a Birth Certificate, also your Straw Man, until the day they issue you a Death Certificate (Straw Man,) you are considered nothing but chattel to your secret slave owners. This is why Dorothy meets "her" "Straw Man" first! The scarecrow/strawman is stuffed with nothing, but hay and rags made to appear real, but he is not. He is a fictional character that has taken the place of the real or higher self you. This is why the Scare Crow is searching for a brain because he has no knowledge of the light spectrum that uses the legal system to enslave him. He is ignorant and dumb to the fact that he is far from free and has been a slave all his life! This lower-level version of yourself is stuck in "hell" with no knowledge how to escape. This is why he has "sea legs" and can barely keep himself upright. He has no foundation to stand on in regard to obtaining knowledge of self from which to free himself from. The title of his theme song is very telling it's called, "If I only had a brain." Coincidently, the Black version of the Wizard of Oz entitled, "The Wiz," the scarecrow is played by Michael Jackson, and its theme song is appropriately named, "You can't win and you can't get out of the game."

- The next character Dorothy meets on the way to following her heart in search of meeting her higher self is the Tin Man. The Tin Man is cold and made of metal. The Tin Man has no feelings, empathy or compassion and chops down living trees not knowing the damage to the world he inflicts. He does not know his lifestyle is predicated on the death and destruction of the world that is kept from him. He is logical, cold and calculating. He only sees the world in terms of his lower self, the world where you only recognize and acknowledge which you can only see, touch, taste, hear or smell. He is a paid employee whose only goal is to pay rent, feed his family, obtain shelter, transportation and clothing. He is motivated by self-survival, which is the lowest level of consciousness one can descend to. When Dorothy finds him, he is rusted shut in a frozen state not able to move or help himself. This is why the Tin Man is in search of a heart. The heart is the first level of higher consciousness. He has never really acknowledged his heart or let alone listened to it or followed it. He has always been concerned and preoccupied with greed and his own self-survival. Following your heart means giving up those addictions and comfort zone that make us feel "safe" and keep us from stepping out on faith and overcoming our fears. The Heart Chakra is the first level of higher consciousness. This is why his theme song is, "If I only had a heart."

- The next character Dorothy meets on her way to discover her higher self and being free is the "Cowardly Lion." The Cowardly Lion doesn't know his own strength. He doesn't believe in himself. He doesn't step out of his comfort zone when he is confronted with adversity. He is a coward through and through even when other people can see the strength within him, he doesn't see it in himself. He is of low self-esteem and a product of a fear-induced environment. The Cowardly Lion represents Dorothy's fragile psyche. She has been conditioned to live and be motivated by fear as a means of control and manipulation by the Powers That Be. Since she doesn't know her own strength, her higher self, she doesn't question authority and will always fall in line with the status quo presented to her as her reality. She will never rise and fight for freedom she doesn't know she never had in the first place. In Dorothy's journey to following her heart she is going to need the courage and bravery housed in her higher self that she never knew she had in the first place. This is why all mighty Lion has been reduced to a shell of himself, his lower self, and is looking for courage, he never knew he already had. His famous quote in the movie is. "How do you make a king out of a slave? Answer: Courage." His theme is, "If I only had the nerve."
- Ultimately, Dorothy makes it to Oz, her higher self, and is met with a stern, all-powerful and menacing figure named the "Wizard of Oz." It is no coincidence that the city of Oz is referred to as the "Emerald City." Emeralds are a shade of green. Green is the color of the Heart Chakra, representing your "Higher Self." It is her dog Toto or the god Anpu that literally pulls the curtain back to reveal the all-knowing, all-powerful Wizard is just a feeble, old white man using smoke and mirrors to perpetuate the myth of his strength and power. The system that enslaved her was only a

façade of illusions made from the electro-magnetic light spectrum controlled by Lucifer, the wizard, that really had no true power. The only power the system had was duping Dorothy into believing she needed it in the first place. Dorothy finally realizes that she had everything she needed within herself and voluntarily gave her power to a system that always meant to enslave her and kept her from her higher self and escaping "Hell." Notice the escape plan in the movie was getting on a hot air balloon and rising above the simulated world. This represented raising your consciousness to your higher self.

- The movie finally reveals to Dorothy that she had to ability to "go home" (her higher self) and escape Hell any time she wanted to. This reveals that Dorothy finally transcended into her higher self which was kept from her by a system of illusions, manipulations and lies that had enslaved her since birth. Reaching your "higher" spiritual self is the key to freedom and the only way to achieve that is overcoming your ego, fears and insecurities and follow the "yellow brick road," that leads to your heart.

The author of the Wizard of Oz

Frank L. Baum was a Luciferian that believed Lucifer fell from heaven to raise mankind. He incorporated Satanist Doctrine by covertly labelling the Wicked Witch of the West as Dorothy's secret savior! Dorothy ultimately makes it to the City of Oz otherwise known as Emerald City. Oz signifies Dorothy's higher self-located in her green heart chakra. At the gate of the city, she is met with a stern and menacing figure at the entrance guarding the gate to the city. It is no coincidence that the same actor who plays the Wizard of Oz, also plays the gatekeeper at the Oz entrance. He also plays the fortune teller in the beginning of the movie and the carriage driver in Oz that controls Dorothy's movements. Being the guard at the entrance of the wizard of Oz's Palace, he decides who was let in and who was turned away. The great and all-powerful wizard of oz is the head slave master that uses smoke and mirrors to convince you to accept your brainwashing and programming by fearmongering. It is her dog Toto, who represents Dorothy's spiritual intuition that literally pulls the curtain back on the system to expose the all-knowing all-powerful wizard is just a feeble, old white man using smoke and mirrors to perpetuate a myth of his strength and power. The system that enslaves Dorothy is really a facade of Illusions conjured up from insecure Europeans that have low self-esteem issues rooted in egotistical narcissism. Once discovered, the wizard gives Dorothy an alternative escape plan to go home in his hot air balloon. Just before they're about to launch, she specifically tells the Scarecrow or her "straw man" that she is going to miss him the most out of all of them. Since her birth, she has been married to her false identity that she has accepted as her true self. Although he was created to enslave her, she feels nostalgic in her dysfunctional relationship with him. Escaping in the hot air balloon symbolizes rising above the simulated world by raising your consciousness to be free. Dorothy's dog Toto sees through the plan and jumps out of the hot air balloon basket pretending to chase a cat in the audience. His action causes Dorothy to chase him. Needless to say, Dorothy misses out as the balloon flies away without her. Toto or Dorothy's higher intuition, understood for the second time that there are no shortcuts to achieving higher levels of consciousness. The only power the system ever had was duping Dorothy into believing that she needed something outside of herself to be complete. The big secret they don't want you to know is they need you more than you need them. He promised you peace and all he demanded in return was your silent obedient consent. Dorothy finally realizes that she had everything she needed within herself. She involuntarily gave up her power by feeding her into her fears and traumas. The system that was intentionally meant to enslave her kept her from achieving the best that she can become. The movie finally reveals to Dorothy that she had the ability to go home or attain her higher self by embracing her heart chakra anytime she wanted. This reveals that Dorothy finally transcended into self-love which was kept from her by a system of Illusions fear manipulation and lies. She was brainwashed since birth reaching her higher self is the key to her freedom. The only way to achieve this is by overcoming your ego, fears and insecurities. Follow the gold or yellow brick road that leads to your heart's destiny. Remember in the beginning, I mentioned the author of The Wizard of Oz, L. Frank Baum was a Luciferian occultist who practiced Satanism. He believed that without Satan, man would lead a mundane life and never reach its full potential. In this movie, Satan or Lucifer is represented by the Wicked Witch of the West. It is no coincidence that one of the most popular and critically acclaimed Broadway musicals called, Wicked is based on a backstory about how the Wicked Witch of the West became evil. She was once good at heart but was always misunderstood because she was different. This is a subliminal message to unknowingly worship Satan. I will give you examples in the movie that further support this theory. Elvira or the Wicked Witch of the West actually plays an important role on Dorothy's journey as she tries to kill Dorothy's lower self so that she can be resurrected. Once this is accomplished, Dorothy's so-called "superpowers" will be bestowed upon her. The Wicked Witch's real name, Elivira, symbolizes new beginnings new opportunities and a chance to start a new life. In one scene, Toto, Dorothy and her straw man stumble upon an apple orchid. In the shadows, we see the Wicked Witch of the West secretly leaving the scene without Dorothy knowing it. They antagonize an apple tree to throw apples at them so that they can eat them which it does. The symbol of the apple, in biblical times represents knowledge. Eve was tricked to bite the apple by Satan who disguised himself as a snake. Dorothy partaking of the apple symbolizes another degree of knowledge she has ascended to on her way to self-discovery. The fact that we see the witch leave the scene right after Dorothy arrives suggests that she set the whole thing up. Is the Wicked Witch of the West secretly helping

Dorothy find her way to Enlightenment even though she seems to be her enemy?

In another scene, the Wicked Witch of the West sends flying monkeys to abduct Dorothy. The symbol of the baboon in ancient Kemet was considered a symbol of knowledge, wisdom and understanding. The way the baboon sits when he is resting resembles a man in deep thought. The ancients made a direct correlation between the baboon and higher consciousness. Also in Kemet, the symbolism of wings or birds are symbols of humanity achieving higher levels of consciousness. They observed birds' ability to fly over obstacles and dangers rather than traverse through them by having to walk through them. The bird symbolism was associated with having higher consciousness by avoiding the mundane traps that exist in living a lower-level existence of self-survival. The flying monkeys helped Dorothy traverse the pitfalls of her mortality by capturing her and flying her to the witch's castle, by avoiding all obstacles in her path. The flying monkeys did Dorothy a favor by transporting her closer to her destiny.

The flying monkey's uniform contains red and white shapes and stripes. As we mentioned earlier, these are the colors of the ancient Kemetic god Heru. His name is where we get the word hero from. The flying monkeys weren't trying to harm Dorothy but on the contrary, they were escorting her on the path to becoming her own hero. The Wicked Witch of the West name, Elvira, can be interpreted as, one who obtains truth or enlightenment by navigating a perilous road. Her skin is the color green, which is the same color as the heart chakra, the first level of higher consciousness. Even the witch's personal guards are called "winky guards." They also have green skin and wear red and white uniforms to symbolize the hero's consciousness Dorothy needs to ascend to. Although they are supposedly the wicked witch's captives, they are forced to serve her. They recite a particular chant that can be translated as, "All we own we owe to her." This is not the chant of an army that is oppressed. The fact that they are named "Winky" guards suggests that there's a hidden meaning or inside joke that only the initiate knows about the guard's true meaning. The gesture of winking of one's eye suggest privileged information being relayed and only known by a select few or those who have been initiated.

The Wicked Witch of the West specifically tries to kill the Scarecrow on three separate occasions. The first time is when Dorothy meets the Tin Man. The witch hurls a fireball at the Scarecrow from a top of rooftop and catches him on fire. Dorothy and the Tin Man have put him out in order to save him. The second time is when the Wicked Witch sent her flying monkeys to capture Dorothy. The monkeys complete their task by capturing Dorothy but also go out of their way to pull the Scarecrow's stuffing apart in an effort to eliminate him. It is the Cowardly Lion and Tin Man that must put him back together again. The last time the wicked witch goes out of her way to kill the Scarecrow is right before Dorothy kills her. The wicked witch lights her broom on fire with a torch and lights the Scarecrow's arm on fire. Right before she sets him on fire, she tells Dorothy, "The last to go we'll see the first three go before her and her mangy little dog too." The reason the wicked witch specifically attacks the Scarecrow is because he is the main reason keeping Dorothy from being free. He is her Straw Man that represents her in a system that enslaves her. In order for Dorothy to escape her prison and reach her higher self, he must be eliminated. Once he is eliminated, she can focus on the other two characters that represent her obstacles that get in the way of her Freedom. The second obstacle represented by the Tin Man is following her heart's intelligence. The third obstacle is her lack of Courage represented by the Cowardly Lion. When Dorothy finally completes her journey and enters the kingdom of Oz she looks up in the sky to see the wicked witch riding on her broomstick spelling out in black smoke coming from her exhaust. The message spells out, "Surrender Dorothy!" In Buddhist philosophy the act of surrendering and having no attachment is the road to enlightenment and higher consciousness. This is another clue that the Wicked Witch of the West was actually helping Dorothy achieve her enlightenment. This is the same concept Satanists believe that Lucifer is actually saving humanity. Dorothy kills the wicked witch by dumping water on her that causes her to melt. The wicked witch cries out as she is dying, “Look what you have done to me?! Oh what a world! What a world! Who would have thought a good little girl like you could destroy mt beautiful wickedness!” Throughout antiquity, spirituality around the world water has always represented a rebirth and a washing away of your sins or a spiritual purification or transformation. The wicked witch describes her wickedness as beautiful because it was the motivator to inspire Dorothy to discover those things in herself that she thought she was lacking. Once you start to accept your pain, traumas, abuse and disappointments as lessons to learn from to become better and not stuck in your own victimization and self-pity. The sooner you will free yourself from your invisible prison that you unknowingly take everywhere you go. Let me break down the opening statement of the movie and I quote:

“For nearly 40 years this story has given faithful service to the young at heart and time has been powerless to put its kindly philosophy out of fashion. To those of you who have been faithful to it in return and to the young in heart we dedicate this picture.”

Let us translate to what this is actually saying. The number 40 in biblical numerology implies some sort of test or judgment so right off the bat there is a struggle that we are facing that are unaware of. Then we get the word, “young” which is capitalized. The word Young can be interpreted as naïve, gullible or vulnerable like innocent sheep being led to slaughter. The word “Heart is also capitalized. It suggests compassion, empathy, nurturing and selflessness. These character traits are exploited and taken advantage of by your secret slave masters. The word “Time” is also capitalized. This suggests that the system they set in place is built for eternity. It is built to last forever. It will never change. The system is not broken or does not need to be fixed it is operating at an optimal level doing what is was designed to do. That's to enslave humans. There's also the word "Fashion." This movie will never be out of fashion. Meaning as long as the system is in place and invested in behind-the-scenes humans will forever be made slaves. This is not a fluke. This is how it's set up to be. it also says, "faithful to it in return." This means those who participate and invest in the conspiracy will always reap the benefits of the masses enslavement. The ones who can keep the secret of this diabolical system will forever be rewarded and protected. "To the young in heart we dedicate this picture." This movie was made for the masses to keep you in servitude." Your ignorance, gullibility and fear are weapons used against you without your knowledge. This system was made to enslave you. In conclusion, I want to leave you with the line from the cowardly lion that has the answer to your emancipation. "What makes a king out of a slave?" Answer, "Courage

In conclusion, I want the reader to put together all the coincidences and parallels associated with the Light Spectrum, mythologies of Lucifer in the Bible, the Vedic chakra system and the concept of the rainbow I have laid out for you. To my surprise, I never knew all the lower-level connotations and references to the rainbow symbolizing and being associated with serpents, death, curses, chaos, disease, destruction and the like. Even in the media and entertainment industries have this symbolism prevalent throughout our culture, as I noted the iconic album cover by Pink Floyd and the first major motion picture filmed in color, The Wizard of Oz. These symbols speak to our subconscious in deciphering the codes to piece all these things together. Lucifer having the nickname, "Bearer of Light." Having "fell" or "kicked out" of heaven which to me can be interpreted as, starting from a higher frequency and descending to a lower frequency of existence. This lower frequency of light being the physical simulation created from a miniscule sliver of energy in the Universe called the Electro-Magnetic Light Spectrum, which coincidently looks like a rainbow. This light spectrum can only be detected by our limited human senses of smell, taste, touch, hear and sight. By humans only relying on these five senses, we have been conditioned to accept this simulation as tangible or physical although we know there is over 99% of energy around us that we are literally blind and oblivious to. In this realm, there are nefarious forces that are hell bent on keeping our souls here by any means necessary when it comes to spiritual transformation. These tactics involve manipulating us to define ourselves by our lowest, animalistic nature to trap our spirits here with no means or knowledge to literally get out of our own way. The main weapon used in this realm to accomplish this task is to coerce us to be motivated by fear by any means necessary. Fearmongering is the most powerful weapon in this simulation. Fear has a slower and lower vibration than its opposite, love. Love is the emotion or "energy in motion" that we must ascend to for our spirits to gather enough velocity to escape the spiritual grave called (gravity.) This way we never find the "exit door" out of this physical simulation and are doomed and cursed to repeat it as we are given life sentences repeatedly upon our reincarnation into this realm. This is why the properties and characteristics of our hearts are misconstrued, downplayed or flat out kept hidden from us. Ancient Vedic, chakra systems and its color-coded blueprint of human consciousness is another clue about having knowledge of self and more importantly a spiritual GPS that pinpoints where your spirit/consciousness is at and how to navigate to find your way out of here. We must literally separate ourselves from our "Lower Self," our animalistic nature that Lucifer conditions us to define ourselves by. From our "Higher Self" or humans defining yourselves as spiritual beings having a temporary human experience from which to learn to transcend from.

The Dark Side of the Moon, an album by the renowned British band Pink Floyd, is a profound exploration of themes that reflect the human condition. I was led to this album because of the artwork of the prism separating the white light into the light spectrum. My path has led me here to explore the hidden meanings and symbols of this album to further collect more clues to the truth of our human condition. Why would a rock band produce an album with this eclectic symbolism in its simplicity? I will unravel the metaphysical meanings embedded within the album, pertaining to money, war, greed, time, death, and mental illness, among others that are associated with rehabilitating, human existence on Earth. Each song offers a reflective examination of the realities we are bound to yet barely comprehend. An existential tangle of consciousness that keeps us tethered to this physical world I relate to the light spectrum.

Regarded as one of the most critically acclaimed records in history and the most profound album cover of all time in its simplicity. The album manifests a collective unconsciousness filled with questions about existence, inner demons, and the societal structures that dominate our lives. The fact that it consistently features in professional listings of the greatest albums of all time is a testament to its enduring relevance and universal resonance. I believe the fascination with this album and it's cover speaks directly to our subconscious about our place in this lower frequency realm. We all have a sixth sense that something is not right in our existence here and that whatever we do, suffering is inevitable and always seems to be our destination.

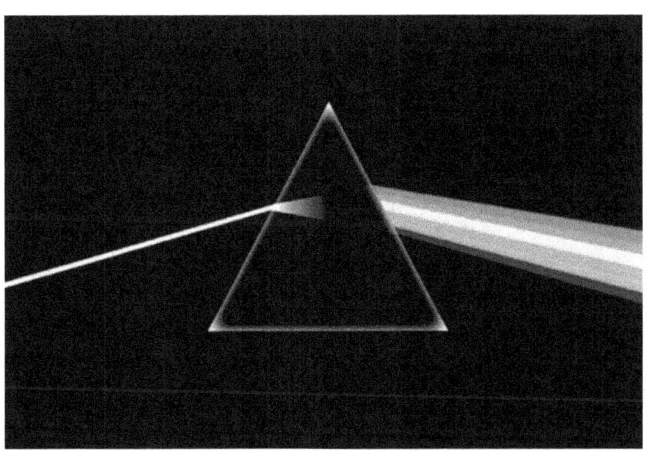

Pink Floyd's 1973 album Dark Side of the Moon.

- The Dark Side of the Moon album addresses and sheds light on themes such as money, war, greed, time, death and mental illness. The subject matter is exclusively addressing the consciousness that keeps us locked into this existence with the notion of never escaping. They are describing the consciousness that one "falls" into to experience "Hell."
- Considered arguably, the greatest album cover of all time. Again, such a simple image on the cover somehow captures the imagination of all those who look at it. At a subconscious level the viewer is seeing a truth which they do not consciously understand. But it is there for all to see hiding in plain sight.
- The Rainbow Theatre in London, where The Dark Side of the Moon was played for the press in 1972 to mark its debut. It is not a coincidence that the place that this album is released and given to the world has a name called, The Rainbow Theater to coincide with Lucifer's Prism (prison) that separates light in this realm to create the electromagnetic light spectrum or rainbow, we call the physical dimension.
- We can never witness the dark side of the moon. That side of the moon is never exposed or seen by people on Earth, suggesting a hidden agenda that humans will always be in the dark about and have no clue as to what is being done to them. You are in Hell, trapped in a prism of light that keeps you locked in your cells, by a prism warden called Lucifer. While you serve a life sentence over and over again.

No.	Title	Artist	Metaphysical Meaning
1.	'Speak to Me'	Nick Mason	The title of this song eludes to the Ego's voice inside people's heads that never goes away. It is motivated by fear and self- survival. The Ego/Lucifer keeps you trapped in "Hell."
2.	'Breathe' (In the Air)	Richard Wright David Gilmour	Breathing consists of Inhaling and Exhaling. When we take our first breath we know we are In Hell/Inhale. When we take our last breath, we know we are Exiting Hell/Exhale.
3.	'On the Run'	Waters Gilmour	From the cradle to the grave, we are born into servitude. The system is stacked against us from the moment we are born. All our lives we are playing catch up but never quite able to ever get ahead.
4.	'Time'	Waters Gilmour Wright Mason	Time is something that this system uses against us. It is an illusion that keeps us trapped in the hamster's wheel going nowhere. Time is used to weakened humanity by arbitrary deadlines that causes us undue stress and strife that keeps us in self-survival mode.
5.	'The Great Gig in the Sky'	Wright Clare Torry	The song is about death and dying and has a profound vocal as if someone is wailing and is grieving profusely. Very somber yet powerful view of humanities consciousness in Hell.

19:15

No.	Title	Music	Metaphysical Meaning
6.	'Money'	Waters:	Very simple, money is the energy that fuels the system that keeps people in a lower state of consciousness. The more you get, the more you want thinking it will solve all your problems.
7.	'Us and Them'	Wright:	This song is about the war that is declared on humanity that pits us against each other in a divide and conquer strategy. Never able to get a chance to look outside the illusion not motivated by fear.
8.	'Any Colour You Like'	Gilmour: Mason Wright	Paying homage to the light spectrum ruled by Lucifer the Light Bearer. They elude that there is actually one color and that's blue. Like in having "the blues." Represents lower level consciousness of mourning.
9.	'Brain Damage'	Waters:	About the issue of mental illness and health that effects all humanity. Mental illness is the number one issue of humanity. From it stems, addiction, dysfunction, homelessness, criminality, ego and hopelessness.
10.	'Eclipse'	Waters:	In this world, no matter what you do it is controlled by Lucifer. There is no escaping while you are here and every experience in this life is attributed to his rule. No one can escape while we are here. An eclipse symbolizes the true light that can never be seen in this realm.

"For our struggle is not against flesh and blood, but against the rulers, against the authorities, against the powers of this dark world and against the spiritual forces of evil in the heavenly realms."

-Ephesians 6:12

The image below is the inside of the album cover. It suggests the "lifeline" of human consciousness that is located in the green, heart chakra. Embracing this frequency is the only way to escape Hell. Notice the green line representing the heart, is the only line in the rainbow that has a pulse, which represents life. All other colors are flatlined, signifying the secret death humans have in this realm called, "Hell." You are the "Walking Dead" and don't even realize it.

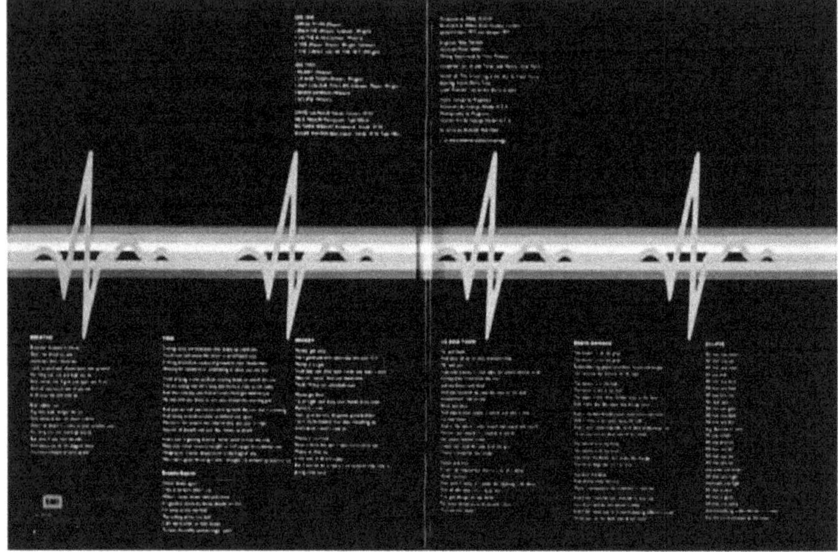

CHAPTER SIX

The Devil Made Me Do It

The Exceptional Love Affair of Zeus and Europa

The Dictionary of Classical Mythology explains that the Greek god, Zeus was enamored by the goddess Europa and decided to "seduce" her which is code for "rape" in European mythology. He transformed himself into a tame white bull and mixed in with her father's herd. While Europa and her helpers were gathering flowers, she saw the bull, caressed his flanks, and eventually got onto his back. Zeus took that opportunity, ran to the sea, and swam, with her on his back, to the island of Crete. He then revealed his identity, and Europa became the first queen of Crete. Zeus gave her a necklace made by Hephaestus and three additional gifts: the bronze automaton guard Talos, the hound Laelaps, who never failed to catch his quarry, and a javelin that never missed. Zeus later re-created the shape of the white bull in the stars, which is now known as the constellation of Taurus.

Here is my metaphysical translation of this Greek mythology story:

The goddess Europa represents the "white" woman of the European race. Through her womb holds and is the gateway for the ancient, genetic code for the white race, known as Euro-peans. Eurpoa can only produce white offspring with her white male counterpart because of their recessive gene pool. She holds the lineage in her DNA of the race of people who classify themselves as white or European today. Her womb or "white" lineage has been "commandeered" by the god Zeus, otherwise known as the Devil, disguised as a Bull. The bull in Greek mythology is also associated with Satan or the devil, as they both possess horns and a powerful animalistic nature. The white race or European were exclusively, chosen by Lucifer to do his bidding in this dimension. This is why European bloodlines are so critical in secret societies. Another name for Lucifer is the god Zeus. Zeus is also known as, "The light shining from the heavens" (aka Lucifer, the Light Bearer.) Zeus "kidnaps" the goddess Europa, whose name translates to, "One with broad or wide eyes."

Europa- Greek (Eurṓpē) contains the elements **(eurus), "wide, broad" and (opt)"eye, face, countenance."**

Translation: One whose eyes are wide open. Metaphysically speaking**, "One who sees through the illusion, of Lucifer's light spectrum!"**

Zeus disguises himself as a **"white bull."** This shows Lucifer's favor to the white race as well as showing his **"horns" as a bull/devil.** The color white can be defined as the absence of color. In this instance, it means seeing through the illusion of the light color spectrum. If one were to get rid of all the colors, there would be no illusion. There would be no electromagnetic light spectrum. Thus, you would see through the lie. Ninety-nine percent of all energy in the Universe is undetected by the five senses human beings possess.

Lucifer, specifically isolates and exalts the European race and proclaims them as his "chosen people." These are the European families or bloodline that control the world in secrecy. This is where you get the secret societies and Illuminati. This is the Genesis of white supremacy! Zeus/Lucifer proceeds to tell elite and powerful Europeans about the realm he has created through his illusion and manipulation of the electromagnetic light spectrum. Once Lucifer tells the white race elites, that they are in Hell, he proceeds to appoint their secret societies as his "gatekeepers" of his realm. With the Illuminati doing his bidding for him, the white race will forever find favor in their position of authority and illusionary "superior" white physical features. Lucifer gives them their ultimate weapon to secure their power and to make sure it will never be taken from them. The "all powerful" weapon that Lucifer gave the European to unleash "Hell" against the majority darker, indigenous people in his realm was, "The Diabolical Science of White Supremacy!"

Wall painting - Europa and the bull - Pompeii (IX 5 18-21) - Napoli MAN 111475 - 02.jpg

The Myth of Europa and How Europe Got its Name. Credit: Following Hadrian/ Wikimedia Commons CC BY-SA 2.0

Lucifer, 2000 years ago, promised Europeans dominion over this dimension if they vowed to serve him. They are now doing his bidding to spread white supremacy throughout the world by spreading racism, sexism, hate, chaos, war, degradation, pillaging and confusion throughout the world to promote as much fear frequency they can to satisfy their god and master. They have taken over politics, the arts, sciences, nutrition, religion, education, entertainment, the economy, sports and medicine. The more fearmongering, they can unleash on unsuspecting native people, the more their master is happy with their undertaking. Unbeknownst to them, they have signed their enslavement as well. The perks they have sold their souls for are the illusion of the value in their white recessive gene pool privilege. As the darker peoples of the world suffer under white supremacy, Europeans suffer from their conspiracy of secrecy and hidden inferiority complex, thus no matter how much they gain in this world they will never be happy or satisfied. The Devil always promises you the world but gives you nothing in return but his illusion, as you sell your soul. The perceived value of European's white skin is also just an illusion. It is really a recessive gene defect of a weaker nature in the human family's genetics. Coincidently, Lucifer appointed them the epitome or the standard of beauty, intelligence, wealth, health, spirituality/religion, society, talent, commerce, politics and even made God in there and Lucifer's image. This is the blond hair, blue eyed Jesus. For as long as their white skin privilege has "perceived" value in this realm, they will never truly try to go against or "fix" the system that Lucifer has installed and presented to them. One thing about making a deal with the devil and selling your soul is the European's soul can never leave this dimension! That's why the European is hell bent on making or having heaven here on Earth to the detriment to all the darker people of this dimension. The further your skin color is from being white, the more "Hell" you will catch! This is a global phenomenon. Travel around the world and you will see this phenomenon in any country you visit. The lighter your skin is, the better your status will be in that society. Consequently, the darker your skin is, you can rest assure your life is catching the most "hell" on the planet wherever you are!" The closer you are to having European or recessive genetic features, the more privileges you will have in this realm. These features include pale skin, stringy light, straight hair, thin long noses, light eyes, big ears, hairy body, and a cankerous disposition. There is a racist saying that is still rings true today, "If you are white, you are alright. If you are yellow, you are mellow. If your brown stick around and if you are Black, get back!"

Remember in mythology Zeus gave Europa several gifts. One was a necklace made by Hephaestus. The necklace was supposed to give the wearer the eternal beauty of her youth. For Europa, the white woman, this refers to her as always being the standard of beauty for eternity around the world. The white woman will do anything humanely possible to keep herself looking youthful. For she knows her value lies in the illusion of her external appearance. Also, necklaces can also be turned into nooses to symbolize Lucifer's "stranglehold" on you if things do not go his way or you go against his wishes. This necklace also brought great misfortune to all its wearers or owners.

The second gift to Europa given by Zeus was the automated, brass humanoid guard named Talos. He was 30 meters high and protected Europa against invaders. I translate this to the technology to create the industrial military complex mastered by Europeans. They have gained access to unlimited resources about technology and advances in war and weaponry and rule the world with an iron fist like no other before them. From Alexander the great, Napoleon, King Leopold, the Roman Empire, Stalin, Hitler, Mussolini, the British Empire, Communist Russia and now the United States with Trump, they have the greatest industrial military war machine in the history of mankind. Europeans have always prided themselves on having the biggest, most destructive weapons on Earth. This technology is Lucifer's gift to their race to rule his domain.

The third and last gift Zeus gave Europa was the hound named, Laelaps. This dog never failed to catch his prey. The literal translation of the dog's name means Hurricane. I interpret this gift as the European's nature to want to rule, colonize and conquer the world wherever he travels. Like a devastating "Hurricane" he leaves death and destruction whatever landmass he invades. This may also allude to the secret weather control programs like HAARP and others to manipulate earthquakes and natural disasters.

The last gift Zeus gave Europa was a javelin or spear that never missed its target. The occult symbol of the spear is the penis. In this instance the white man's penis. The symbology of the spear refers to the genetic potency of the white man's DNA to dominate all the darker peoples of the world through his weapon of white supremacy. The white man has weaponized his penis as "toxic masculinity" and uses it as a weapon of violence to control, destroy, enslave, and oppress. The white man has made this particular dysfunctional personality type in Lucifer's image. The Malignant Narcissist is the epitome of measured success, power, celebrity, and attractiveness in a man. His overcompensation for his lack of size compared to the African man has made him unsure of himself so he must overcompensate for his lack of sexual prowess. Coincidently, this javelin Zeus gave Europa, never missed its target.

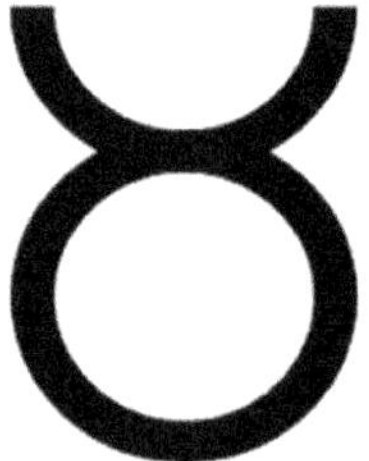

The image on the left is the universal symbol for the devil, the middle image is the zodiac sign for Taurus, which represents Zeus & the picture on the right is the hand signal for the devil's horns in the occult.

The Illuminati symbol in the image above represents a small, faction sworn to secrecy led by Europeans who rule the world in the shadows. They are called the "Illuminated Ones" or those who can "See" through the illusion of light. The image is a triangle which represents the Prism that separates white light to create this dimension. The eye in the middle surrounded by the light spectrum rays symbolizes those who know

Lucifer controls this illusionary realm and have pledged their loyalty to him in secrecy. They are instrumental in creating his heaven here on Earth. Although they get to eat the crumbs that fall from his table, their souls can never leave here. The devil promises you the world but gives you nothing and takes everything.

The image below is a collage of celebrities showing their one eye being open. This sign let's others know that they are initiated in the secret society that worships Lucifer and the truth about this realm has been revealed to them. They have "sold their souls" as part of the initiation that leads to influence, wealth, fame, power, and celebrity.

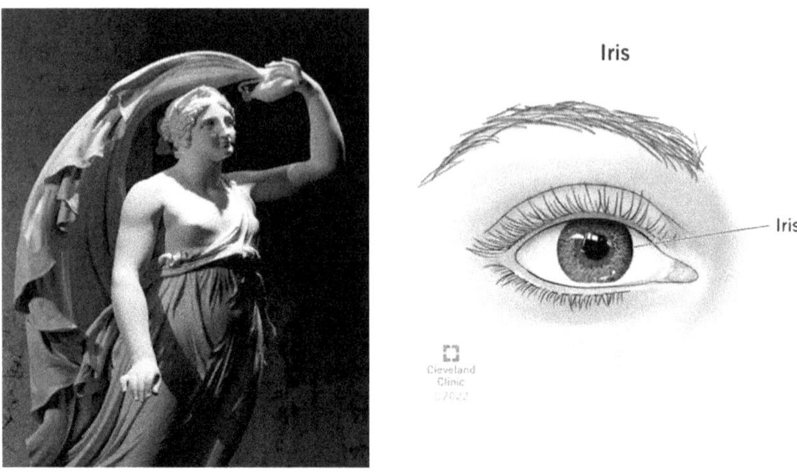

Image on the left is Iris, the goddess of the rainbow, marble sculpture by Italian sculptor Gaetano Matteo Monti, 1841. Kunsthistorisches Museum, Vienna.

Image on the right, in Greek mythology, the goddess Iris was the goddess of rainbows. Notice the cloth over her head representing the light spectrum/rainbow that she has domain under. Iris is also the part of the eye that allows us to see this dimension. Her job was to send messages from the gods to man concerning warfare and retribution. She was a snitch appointed by Lucifer to spread disinformation and chaos in this realm. She also would carry water from the river Styx to the gods. The river Styx runs through a place called Hades, otherwise known as Hell.

The Iris is the colored part of the eye that for Europeans is commonly blue. Blue is the chakra for communication. The question is who and what are they communicating with?!?

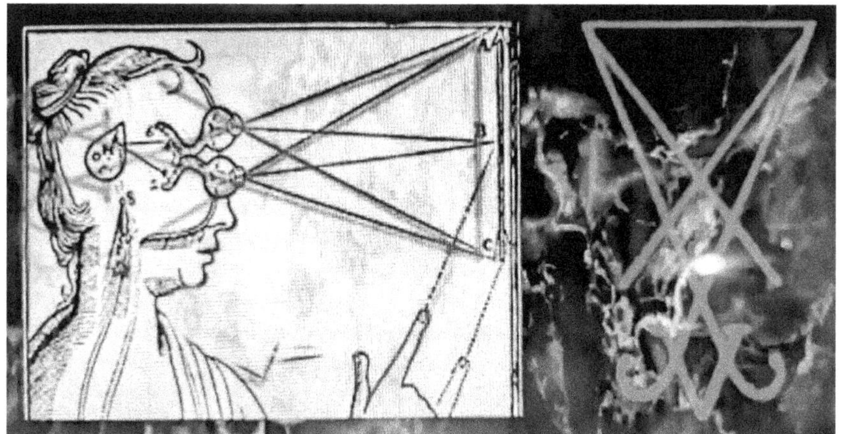

A sigil used in rituals invoking Lucifer, first recorded in the 18th-century True Grimoire. Known among Theistic Satanists as the Seal of Satan.

The image above represents in the occult the devil worshippers, "Seal of Satan." Notice how it relates to human eyeballs as it forms some type of triangulation about the dynamics of human vision or sight. Another clue into the physical illusion and flaws of human vision being manipulated by Lucifer in his Electromagnetic Light Spectrum realm.

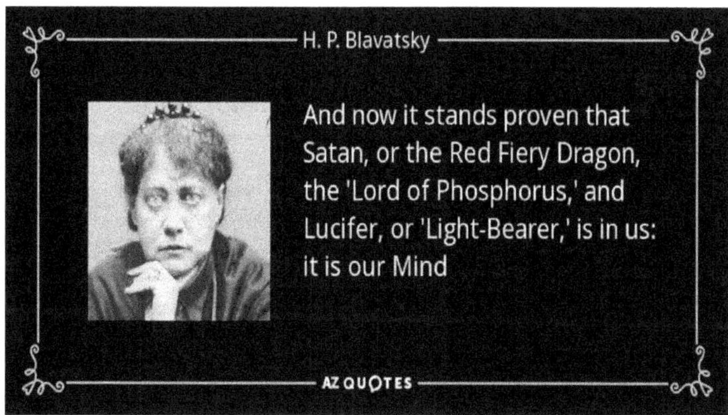

Lucifer came to the world to wake man up, to help him remember his divine origin, the divine origin of his Spirit, and to help him free himself from the body-soul in which he is trapped, and from created time and matter." -Madam Blavatsky

Madame Blavatsky refers to Lucifer as the "Lord of Phosphorus." Phosphorus has the atomic weight of 15 which in numerology comes out to be the number 6 which represents the Biblical "Number of the Beast in Man."

Phosphorus elemental shape shown below is a tetrahedron. The same pyramid shape as the Prism that separates white light to reveal the Electromagnetic Light Spectrum. Phosphorus in the occult has always been associated with Satan, Lucifer or the Devil. In Latin, Phosphorus and Lucifer are equivalent to each other. The etymology of the word Phosphorus comes from the Greek words "phos" (light) and "pherein" (to bear), ie: "The Light Bearer!" Also, in Greek mythology phosphorus is referred to as The Morning Star, "The Dawn Bringer", and associated with Venus, which is also known as "The Morning Star", which is another name for Lucifer in the Bible. The goddess and planet Venus are also associated with the concept of Love. This implies humanity's secret manipulation and worship of the "Love of Lucifer!"

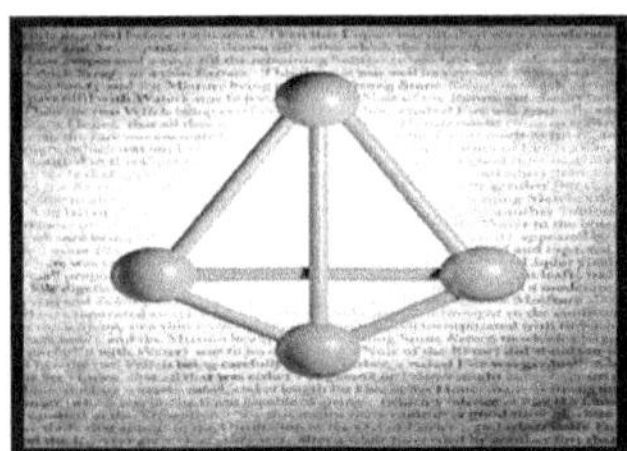
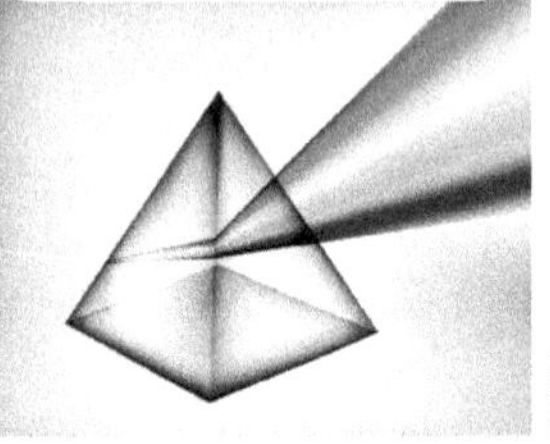

The mysterious Madame Helena Blavatsky was the 19th century's most famous and notorious occultist. She was also the godmother of the "New Age" movement in America. Madame Blavatsky supposedly travelled around the world in countries like, India, Egypt, Asia, America and extensively throughout Europe in search of ancient, secret spiritual knowledge. She studied the mythological seven stages of human evolution called the, "Root Races." This belief is that the Aryan race, or those people classify themselves as "white," with blue eyes and blond hair, were the "master race" of the world. Their superiority was "appointed"

to them by a race of alien beings that possess the same features. I relate her reference to "Alien Beings" to Lucifer and the Fallen Angels. She was the one to give Hitler and the Nazi Movement the Swastika symbol she stole from Eastern philosophy religions. This symbol is a cross that is spinning. When it is represented as a cross spinning clockwise, it is a symbol of life, prosperity and abundance. When it is spinning counterclockwise, like how the Nazis display it, it represents death, destruction and chaos. When she came to the United States, she founded a secret society group called the, Theosophical Society in New York City in 1875. In 1877, she published her book, "Isis Unveiled," which outlined her esoteric worldview. She claimed her book was revitalizing ancient, hermetic wisdom that has been lost or hidden, which has been used as the foundation for all major world religions. The fact that she uses, "Unveiled" in her book title symbolizes to me that European elites hold many secrets that they exclusively share amongst themselves in regard to this realm and the fallen angel Lucifer. The word, "Veil" can be defined as a piece of fine material worn by women to conceal their face. Her foundation and literature were the foundation of the "Luciferian Doctrine" she brought to the United States. This doctrine was adopted by high level, free masons and those who practiced white supremacy as an institution. One of her devotees was a master mason named Albert Pike. He was a general in the Confederate army and was the founder of the Ku Klux Klan, the largest white supremacist terrorist group in North America. Madame Blavatsky's beliefs fueled that the white race was ordained by "alien" beings as the masters of this world. This sounds very familiar when you decipher the Luciferian Doctrine?

"Without Lucifer or Satan man would never evolve to higher consciousness." -Blavatsky

- "We have said that Lucifer came to the world to wake man up, to help him remember his divine origin, the divine origin of his

Spirit, and to help him free himself from the body-soul in which he is trapped, and from created time and matter."

- Yet who can deny that even Jesus is portrayed as boldly proclaiming his identity with Venus the Light bringer in Revelation 22:16, where he says "I, Jesus, am the bright and morning star." If the translators had chosen to translate this verse using Latin just as they did with Isaiah 14:12, it would read "I, Jesus, am Lucifer."

"One of the most hidden secrets involves the so-called fall of Angels. Satan and his rebellious host will thus prove to have become the direct Saviors and Creators of divine man. Thus Satan, once he ceases to be viewed in the superstitious spirit of the church, grows into the grandiose image. It is Satan who is the God of our Planet and the only God. Satan (Lucifer) represents the Centrifugal Energy of the Universe this ever-living symbol of self-sacrifice for the intellectual independence of humanity."

-Helena P. Blavatsky, 32nd Degree Freemason, The Secret Doctrine.

Lucifer THE LIGHT BEARER

New Series, Vol. VII., No. 26. VALLEY FALLS, KANSAS, FRIDAY, DECEMBER [illegible] Whole No. [illegible]

LUCIFER—THE LIGHT-BEARER

PUBLISHED WEEKLY.

Lucifer the Light Bearer was an individualist anarchist journal published in the United States by Moses Harman in the late 19th and early 20th centuries. This was literature for Satanist who called themselves -Luciferians.

Image on the left is Helena Blavatsky, detail of an oil painting by Hermann Schmiechen, 1884; in a private collection Encyclopædia Britannica, Inc. Image on the right is the Baphomet goat assigned to Lucifer. An 1856 depiction of the Sabbatic Goat from Dogme et Rituel de la Haute Magie by Éliphas Lévi. The arms bear the Latin words SOLVE (dissolve) and COAGULA (coagulate). Baphomet's right arm pointing up has the inscription "Dissolve." This means to make less dense as in light as a feather. His left arm has the inscription "Coagula." This means to make more dense or heavier like the state of matter in this material realm that traps us here. I will break down this concept more thoroughly later in the book.

Madame Blavatsky secretly spread throughout the world, her doctrine that Aryan people were ordained as the "stewards" of Lucifer the Light bearer himself. The white race was appointed to maintain his control, mission, power and status quo to subject non-Aryan people in a life of servitude in his realm until they die. In my opinion, this was the birth of the Illuminati in North America. Who are the "Illuminati?" Adam Weishaupt (1748–1830) was the founder of the Illuminati. He started teaching at a Jesuit University in England and was later disenfranchised with their limited teachings and dogma. Weishaupt favored the school of thought of Enlightenment. The Age of Enlightenment or the Age of Luciferian Doctrine was an intellectual and philosophical movement that dominated Europe in the 17th and 18th centuries with global influences and effects. It went beyond the church's teachings and was more scientific, self-impowering and against state or church ultimate power. Its teachings were banned by the church; thus, secret societies were born. Finding secret societies like freemasonry does not open to his school of thought he founded his own secret society called the Illuminati, which literally means, the "Enlightened Ones" or those who can see through the dark. The "dark" I believe they are referring to is the Electromagnetic Light Spectrum. They understood that the physical dimension is made up of lower level frequencies and vibrations otherwise known as the Light Spectrum or Vedic Chakra System. As we referred earlier, this is Lucifer's realm or what the Christians refer to as Hell. I believe that Madame Blavatsky was secretly initiated into the Illuminati and came to the United States as well as other countries around the world to set up secret societies to establish the foundations of a New World Order where Lucifer has domain and is not only worshipped in the shadows but also in the light! Their main objective is to enslave the darker people of this realm and usurp their natural resources. White supremacy is the number one weapon the Illuminati uses to wheel its power with Lucifer's blessing and help. Remember, they believe, their god, Lucifer ordained them as the gatekeepers of this realm. Only Aryan people or people who classify themselves as white can belong to the Elite. When we look further into this concept, we realize the region that these Aryan people come from is called Europe. Europe was named after the goddess Europa, which means "eyes wide open or one who can see in the dark!" These elite,

Aryan people are the ones who know this hidden knowledge and use the Luciferian philosophy and magic to rule the world in the shadows of the light spectrum. Also, the Roman counterpart god that is related to Zeus is named Jupiter. Coincidently, the planet Jupiter has a moon named, you guessed it, Europa!

The picture of Donald Trump, on the left, taking the "oath" to become the President of the United States. Notice the Freemason god Baphomet, in the picture on the right, is giving the same pose or stance. The right hand pointing up signifies the promotion of lower consciousness housed in the left hemisphere of the brain, and the left arm pointing down symbolizes the suppression of higher consciousness housed in the right hemisphere of the brain. This is the conspiracy that secret societies implement to control and manipulate the masses into embracing their lower consciousness, while at the same time, never letting them acknowledge their higher selves. Anyone that holds a position of wealth, power or influence over the masses must pledge their allegiance to these secret societies first and foremost. You must make a, "deal with the devil." They will only stay in power if they serve their hidden masters and not the common people. If you hold a job position that you are required to take any oath, you have voluntarily given your power away to an entity that does not have your best interests. Thus, you have, "Sold your soul!"

Everyone in position of power, wealth, authority or influence must take the oath and serve their god, Baphomet, the free mason god, who represents Lucifer. There is no other way.

"Ye are of your father the devil, and the lusts of your father ye will do. He was a murderer from the beginning, and abode not in the truth, because there is no truth in him. When he speaketh a lie, he speaketh of his own: for he is a liar, and the father of it." -John 8:44

The Mythology of the Morning Star

There are two entities associated with the name, "Morning Star." Lucifer being one and the planet Venus being the other. On a side note, Maia Morgenstern who played Jesus' mother, Mary in the film, "The Passion of the Christ," last named literally means, "Morning Star." Consequently, she also played a woman who was brutally raped in the movie preceding her Jesus's mother role of Mary. Now that is diabolical!

Let's get into the goddess Venus mythology of the Roman goddess of Love, beauty, sex and fertility. The Greeks called her Aphrodite. She was also the patron saint of prostitutes, but her main characteristic was Love. According to the myth, Venus married the god of war, Mars. This seems like a contradiction. How can the goddess of Love be attracted to and marry the god of war? Let's continue the contradiction. She had many children from different gods. With the god Mars, she gave birth to Timor (Phobos.) He was the personification or god of Fear who accompanied his father into battle. His twin brother was the god Metus (Deimos.) He was the embodiment or god of Terror. So how does the goddess of Love be attracted to and marry the god of War and have twin sons who represent Fear and Terror? Venus even gave birth to the god Cupid from another god named Mercury. Mercury was the god of commerce, trickery and thieves. Cupid is the god of love, symbolized as a baby (pedophilia?) He has an arrow, as a weapon that causes pain and can kill. Remember, what realm we are in. We reside in a lowly place where Lucifer rules over us. Lucifer uses unseen energy and our lowest, human nature against us. He is all about the illusion of perception and not substance. He is about sleight of hand and misdirection. He thrives in a world of confusion and chaos and uses his cunning to deceive us. He uses language to manipulate and control us as he lurks in the shadows of this world directly out of sight of our senses.

Let me let you in on the world's biggest hoax. In the human body, emotions (energy in motion) of Love and fear express themselves by the exact same physical characteristics. Lucifer designed it to confuse humanity into thinking Fear is to be loved and Love is to be feared. Why do we gravitate towards social media "influencers" who promote ego, show fights, gossip, slander, tragic accidents, flaunt wealth and fake body parts? This is all narcissistic behavior which we will cover shortly. It is all done by design. Because Lucifer has tricked us to Love fear and to fear Love!

As you can see judging only by the physical characteristics of a person's emotions, one cannot be precisely sure if they are experiencing Love or if it's Fear. This is the con Lucifer has played on humanity. He has tricked us into loving and worshiping fear instead of Love. Our human bodies respond the same way to each opposite emotion, so it is easy for him to substitute one for the other! We have become addicted to fearmongering and look at love as a weakness. This is why we slow down on the freeway when there is an accident. We want to witness Fear (Phobos) & Terror (Deimos.) This is why reality TV shows with the most drama and dysfunctional cast members are the most popular shows. This is why we gossip about things that are not uplifting and inspiring or healing. We continually put other people down to feel better about ourselves. We take kind people as weak people and shame them for their kind hearts and trusting nature. We love "Bad Boys" and worship "Bad Bitches." We are masters of looking at each other's weaknesses only to magnify them and exploit them by gossiping to others. This is why they report on the news 95% of tragedies and only 5% of inspirational stories. Because no one would watch if it was the other way around. We have "fallen" in love with fear and cannot get enough of it. We are addicted and crave more every day. This is how a serial sex offender and misogynist, 34 time prosecuted, fraud felon, porn star sleeping, racist, & white supremacist, scammer, best friend of pedophile Jefferey Epstein, grifter, morally bankrupt, compulsive lying narcissist who takes advantage of his own followers and bullies people instead of protecting them, can be voted in as the U.S. President and leader of the free world for a second time!

Identical Physical Characteristics of Emotions Lucifer Manipulates Humans When They Experience Love or Fear to Confuse Them.

- ***Heartbeat increases and flutters.***
- ***Perspiration increases in the palm of the hands, underarms & forehead.***
- ***Mouth becomes extremely dry. I.e. Cotton Mouth***
- ***Voice becomes shaky and trembles or we lose it altogether.***
- ***Knees start to knock and legs start to shake and get weary.***
- ***Butterflies in the stomach.***
- ***Nausea or upset stomach.***
- ***Feeling lightheaded.***
- ***Hard to breathe and can't catch our breath.***
- ***Adrenaline rush.***
- ***Panic attack.***
- ***Hard to move or stuck in our tracks,***
- ***Can't think clearly. Brain fog.***

All these are physical characteristics humans experience whether being in Love or experiencing fear. The devil created our emotions

(energy in motion) that way to confuse humans into worshipping fear and not Love.

Above are two artist renditions of the goddess Venus/Aphrodite. Notice she is naked in both paintings but ashamed of her nakedness. Love is not shameful. Love has no embarrassment because it has no ego. It is pure love. On the right we see a rainbow (light spectrum) shining over the Morning Star, Venus the goddess of Love. On the left image, we see a woman on her right trying to cover the goddess in a multicolored cloth, which I associate the material with the light spectrum. They both represent the light spectrum of Lucifer's domain and how he has subliminally tricked us into thinking love means to fear. Also, the picture on the left above, shows the goddess in a shell, which represents this realm. Notice she is standing on the shores where water and land meets. This signifies the horizon of consciousness where man must decide where he wants to dwell in his spirit. The Water represents the higher self (feminine) and the land represents man's lower self (masculine.) Remember, land or more specifically matter is the illusion Lucifer uses to enslave man.

CHAPTER SEVEN

The Devil Is In the Details

One would be surprised how the brain can be tricked using images and symbols to distort your perception of reality. These are built in flaws in humans that Lucifer exploits to his benefit. There are certain "blind spots" in our visual cortex, so the brain uses assumptions to "fill in the blanks" of our reality based on its previous programming. These blank spots are filled in by Lucifer's ongoing and relentless conditioning and brainwashing. The brain is taking in so much data in a short amount of time so it can be overloaded. If it tried to decipher everything at once at the same time it would short circuit. The brain must make "assumptions" for us as to predict what our reality is programmed to be. These "assumptions" can be manipulated in the shadows. He who controls the images and symbols in our lives, is our slave master and his name is Lucifer. Our behavior is controlled by our subconscious mind without us even knowing it. Our subconscious mind can only decipher images and symbols to communicate with it. It cannot differentiate what is real from what is not. It assumes that it has experienced all things that it has been programmed to accept or exposed to and internalizes it as fact. The subconscious mind controls our behavior based on the perception of these images and symbols it is exposed to. These images and symbols invoke emotions in us or "energy in motion" that motivates our behavior, causing us to "catch feelings" or become traumatized. It is the parasympathetic fight, flight or freeze response we do involuntarily. Our brain focuses on the programmed, "meaning of things" not the actual detail of things in real time. That's why the "Devil is in the details!" This is exactly why multinational corporations pay billions of dollars in their advertising and marketing campaigns annually. Their "brands" enslave us and their "logos" brainwash our minds. Your five senses have been programmed by your masters to deceive and enslave you. You have never questioned the legitimacy of the source that gave you the information that defines your reality. He who rules makes the rules. He who controls the images and symbols of your reality becomes your slave master. This is because images and symbols speak directly to your subconscious mind. Your subconscious mind controls over 90% of your behavior without you even knowing it. Are you thinking your thoughts or are your thoughts thinking you?

"Whoever controls the image and information of the past will determine what and how future generations will think; and, whoever controls the information and images of the present, will also determine how these same people will view the past."
- George Orwell, author of the book

Other scientifically diagnosed shortcomings of the human brain that Lucifer exploits in humans.

- **Inattentional Blindness**- an individual fails to perceive an unexpected stimulus in plain sight, purely because of a lack of attention rather than any vision defects or deficits. When it becomes impossible to attend to all the stimuli in each situation, a temporary "blindness" effect can occur, as individuals fail to see unexpected but often salient objects or stimuli. This is where Lucifer manipulates your behavior behind the curtain, in the shadows and "fills in the blanks" for you! You are not crazy. You are under the influence of an entity that means to enslave you with invisible whips and chains! The devil made you do it as he lurks and tempts you in the shadows of your perceived reality!

- **Change Blindness**- a perceptual phenomenon that occurs when a change in a visual stimulus is introduced and the observer does not notice it. For example, observers often fail to notice major differences introduced into an image while it flickers off and on again like a strobe light. It is this defect in our vision where Lucifer exploits us. This is equivalent to "spiking your drink" without you even knowing it to take full advantage of you. You are constantly, "under the influence!" Seeing may be believing, but believing may not always be the truth. Your belief is Lucifer's deceit!
- **The goal of human vision** is not to take in every detail in the world and correlate it to the mind, the goal of vision is to make sense of the world around you in real time. "Making sense" means to justify the programming and conditioning of your traumatic past that Lucifer infiltrated your mind that is based on past fear and trauma. In this way, you become predictable and thus his slave. Every future action you do will always be based on your past fears and you will always be in a perpetual loop of survival. If you are in a constant state of fear, your mind is incapable of making rational decisions. Your decision making will be based on your fleeting emotions that can and will be easily manipulated by him. Thus, your decisions become predictable as they will always be predicated on your emotional manipulation of your unseen master.
- **The goal of Lucifer** in this realm is to control human's attention and never let go of it from the cradle to the grave. This is where you get the phrase, "Pay attention." It cost you your life and is very expensive. You are groomed to be a slave from day one by his use of media broad cast used to cast a spell over you and television programming, used to brainwash you. It is sad today when I see a four-month-old baby hypnotized by their mother's computer

tablet or cell phone. Lucifer creates addicts out of humans from birth. Addicts are easily manipulated and controlled because they will go against their best interests just to get another fix! Fear and chaos are the foundation for the fall of man's consciousness. Thus, violence and trauma are shoved down your throat 24/7, seven days a week in the media.

The most valuable commodity in this realm is not gold, diamonds or even precious metals. It is your "attention span," that you are required to pay your slave master on the daily. This is why data mining to build your personal profile online which is bought and sold like a slave auction, at a premium without your permission! Your online identity consists of your personal psychological profile and demographics like gender, social status, income level, race, sexual preferences, education level, religion, idiosyncrasies, habits, addictions, shortcomings, vices, food preferences, recreational activities, brand preferences and the like. These 1000 points in your online profile create the "Artificial You" or the "Cyber/Slave You," from which Lucifer uses to exploit and imprison. Your online profile or false identity, otherwise known as your Ego, now supersedes your authentic self. It now usurps the power of your "higher self" and takes the place of the "real you" over time in the World Wide Web. Your true or higher self becomes trapped in the web where Lucifer the spider sucks all the lifeforce out your body leaving you with nothing more than an empty shell of yourself. You are now a captive in its web! Now you define yourself by your Ego which feeds your "Artificial Profile" by online programming, conditioning and advertisements, as your authentic self gradually withers away until it becomes non-existent. Like the empty shell of a carcass that a spider has caught in its web and has sucked all the blood out of its prey. You are now Lucifer's personal slave without one whip or chain being implemented. You are unknowingly caught in an invisible web as Lucifer sucks the life force out of your body, mind and soul. You are stuck as an empty shell of the potential person you could have evolved into. Now you are forced fed all your addictions, fears and traumas that fill the empty void inside of you where your soul used to dwell.

- **Predicting human behavior** is powerful science that is used to exploit the masses in secrecy. Therefore, chains and whips are no longer needed to make you a slave. There are esoteric, complex scientific, socio-economic, elegant mathematical equations that Lucifer uses to manipulate and coerce humans into doing his deeds. Humans are secretly being exploited as their puppets. You have been conditioned to believe there are no coincidences in life. Lucifer's plan is a long con game, and you humans are oblivious to being his prey. Everything is calculated. Everything is intentional. There are no mistakes in his calculated world and everything in his realm is a Scam!
- **Misdirection**- the action of making people pay attention to the wrong thing, usually intentionally so that they will not notice something else. People are more easily manipulated when they are exposed to fear and chaos. Lucifer will manufacture events to make humans afraid and confused to control them even more. Donald Trump has mastered the art of misdirection. The very thing he says he is fighting against is the very thing he is doing to manipulate his unsuspecting followers. This is called, "Gaslighting." Lucifer's favorite and most powerful manipulation tactic. Get the people to fear a contrived enemy that you say you are fighting against, but "You" are the real enemy and the real threat!
- **The hardest things** for the human eye to see are those things right in front of you. The more things that are familiar to you the more hiding places Lucifer has to exploit. Lucifer hides in plain sight in the shadows and in the blind spots of your subconscious mind. Remember, Lucifer was God's favorite angel because of his stunning beauty, superb intelligence and amazing talent. Don't be deceived! Demons live among you and they are called Narcissist today. They are successful, charming, charismatic, beautiful,

confident, admired and well spoken. But please don't be fooled! Remember, the Devil's ultimate trick is deception and empty promises!

- **When we try** to remember something in real time during conversations, we cannot process new data simultaneously. This leaves us susceptible to manipulation and deception by the person we are listening to. This is why scammers speak so fast when they communicate with you. They purposely "overload" your brain with information so you can't catch up and process the lies they spew at will. This leaves the victim only able to process the truth in the things they say that resonate and the lies become just a blur in their minds. Scammers intentionally overload your brain with data by speaking fast, sprinkle a little truth amongst the lies they spew, create an emotional attachment to the victim and have the confidence and charisma to pull it off by looking and speaking as an authority on the subject. They are nothing more than grifters. Lucifer speaks fast in the hopes of trying to smuggle something by your consciousness, hoping you do not detect his lies and deceptions.
- **Mob mentality**- also called herd or hive mentality -- The inclination that some humans must be part of a large group, often neglecting their individual feelings in the process, and adopting the behaviors and actions of the people around them. The term is used to describe how humans blindly follow the crowd and take on different manners, follow trends and buy merchandise based on their circle of influence. Lucifer just has to control one leader in a group to control the masses that follow him. The concept of mob mentality was first introduced by social psychologists and group think pioneers Gabriel Tarde and Gustave Le Bon in the 1800s. ***[https://www.techtarget.com/whatis/definition/mob-mentality] - Kate Brush***

You know you are a part of a "Mob Mentality" if you are a part of any of these organizations:

1. MAGA
2. Organized Religion
3. Fraternities/Sororities
4. Secret Societies
5. Sports Fans
6. Law Enforcement/Armed Services
7. Manosphere Community
8. Gangs/ Prisoners
9. Cults
10. Social Media Communities
11. Political Party Affiliation
12. Finance/Banking Industry
13. Any organization you belong to that has a specific logo, uniform, color, hand sign or oath.

"Those who manipulate this unseen society constitute an invisible government which is the true ruling power of our country. We are governed, our minds are molded, our tastes formed, our ideas suggested largely by men we have never heard of...in almost every act of our daily lives, whether in the sphere of politics or business, in our social conduct or our ethical thinking we are dominated by the relatively small number of persons... who understand the mental processes and social patterns of the masses. It is they who pull the wires which control the public mind who harness old social forces and contrive new ways to bind and guide the world."

--Edward Bernays (Propaganda.)

Edward Bernays, a pivotal figure in the 20th century and nephew to acclaimed psychologist Sigmund Freud, was often called the "father of public relations." He is most notable for his groundbreaking work in the field of propaganda. Known for his innovative methods, he leveraged psychology and other social sciences to pioneer techniques that influenced public opinion. Bernays believed that understanding the mechanics of the human mind was crucial in swaying public opinion, which subsequently had profound implications on the course of mass communication, marketing, and even politics.

Illusion of Control

Sense of agency refers to the feeling of control over actions and their consequences. As with other aspects of conscious experience, the sense of agency is not an infallible reproduction of objective reality. Because of this our experiences of agency can go awry. This is quite common in gambling, where players often feel an exaggerated sense of agency. An example of just such an illusion of control was noted by Henslin in the 1960s. Henslin was a sociologist and spent several weeks observing cab drivers in St. Louis in the USA. A popular past time among the cabbies was craps, a dice rolling gambling game. Henslin joined in with these games and made an intriguing observation. When these cab drivers came to roll the dice, they altered their behavior depending on the number they needed, throwing harder for higher numbers and more gently for lower numbers. What is striking about this kind of behavior is that the outcome of dice rolling is objectively uncontrollable. Nevertheless, these cabbies clearly felt otherwise. This is an example of where the sense of agency can be quite divorced from objective reality.

- Henslin J. M. (1967). Craps and Magic. Am. J. Sociol. 73 316–330. 10.1086/224479

"When we make voluntary actions we tend not to feel as though they simply happen to us, instead we feel as though we are in charge. The "Sense of Agency" refers to this feeling of being in the driving seat when it comes to our actions."

Our thoughts of being in control are Lucifer's way of conditioning and programming us to do his will, while simultaneously having us think we make all our decisions based on our own free will, which is an illusion.

"In the field of psychology, **"Cognitive Dissonance"** is the perception of contradictory information and the mental toll of it. Relevant items of information include a person's actions, feelings, ideas, beliefs, values, and things in the environment. Cognitive dissonance is typically experienced as psychological stress when persons participate in an action that goes against one or more of those things.

1] According to this theory, when two actions or ideas a person experiences are not psychologically consistent with each other, people do all in their power to change them until they become consistent!

2) The discomfort is triggered by the person's belief clashing with new information perceived, wherein the individual tries to find a way to resolve the contradiction to reduce their discomfort.

-https://en.wikipedia.org/wiki/Cognitive dissonance.

Examples of Cognitive Dissonance are as follows:

- A woman who justifies staying in a long-term relationship with an abusive man thinking he is going to change one day.
- A person not admitting to themselves nor others that they have an addiction problem even when they have lost everything and hit rock bottom.
- A church goer believing their pastor is innocent when his numerous victims speak out against him and show receipts.
- A mother not believing her children when they report back to her that her new boyfriend is sexually abusing them and she blames them for being "fast."

- Giving your money to a person everyone knows is a scammer, but you refuse to believe it because you have invested too much for too long.
- Going to the doctors and he informs you your health is in danger, and you need to change your diet and exercise regularly and you think he is overreacting because you "feel" healthy.
- Thinking your partner wants to marry you after living with them for 10 years with the same person and they never move forward.
- Not believing the number on the scale when you stand on it and blame the scale for being broken or you think it's just "water weight".
- Being at a job for numerous years and they keep making excuses why you haven't been promoted and you continue to stay for the big promotion that never comes.
- Chasing a woman and showering her with money and gifts but she never has time for you even though she tells you she loves you.
- Playing the lottery like clockwork for over 40 years thinking the next drawing will make all your losses worth it so you continue to play week after week losing more money than you will ever win back. Same can be said for playing slot machines or any gaming activity.

Amygdala Hijack

The amygdala is an almond-shaped structure in the brain. It is involved in processing emotions. There are two of these structures: one in each hemisphere of the brain. Both are located near the base.

-Psychologist Daniel Goleman first used the term "amygdala hijacking" in his 1995 book Emotional Intelligence: Why It Can Matter More Than IQ.

It refers to situations wherein the amygdala hijacks control a person's ability to respond rationally to a threat. This then leads to the person reacting in an intense, emotional way that may be out of

proportion to the situation. Without the ability to use their frontal lobes, a person is unable to think clearly. Therefore, they are not in control of their responses. They will always react spontaneously and emotionally which can lead to psychological manipulation by those who know how to "push your buttons."

One of Lucifer's strategies include, "Problem, reaction, solution." Lucifer creates the initial problem, which ignites your programmed reaction that he has conditioned in you. Then he offers his solution to the problem he created to get you to do what he wants in the first place. This is the "Amygdala Hijacking." For example, let's say Lucifer wants you to take a vaccine you otherwise wouldn't take if your mind was thinking properly. He would first create the problem, in this case it would be a deadly, worldwide virus. The reaction he wants you to adopt would be manipulated in the media, which pumps fear into the masses claiming the "disease" is deadlier than it really is and exaggerates the number of deaths caused by it. This causes rampant paranoia amongst the masses of people, which causes them the inability to think and respond rationally. Lucifer knows your programmed reaction would be to voluntarily give up your power to him so he can make the problem go away so you can feel safe again at all costs.

How to get healthy, free people to voluntarily inject a foreign substance into their bodies without a fight.

The Problem: Create a "deadly virus."

The Reaction: People's paranoia of illness & fear of dying propagated by the media.

The Solution: The masses voluntarily take the mandatory vaccine to find a sense of peace.

Mission accomplished! Lucifer creates the "perceived problem." He knows how the people will react according to his programming.

Then he gets them to do something they otherwise would not do in their right minds. His created solution.

The Devil Created Christianity

Before Christianity, there was a growing, Coptic spiritual practice the grew out of Ethiopia but originated from the area presently known as Sudan. This metaphysical practice of searching for God from within, was the blueprint that the present-day religion of Christianity reversed engineered and usurped their religious doctrine from. These divine mystics knew that way out was in. In other words, to escape man's lower nature known as the ego, and come spiritual beings having a human experience, man had to search within himself and master his lower nature through discipline, suffering, high morals and values, integrity, self-sacrifice, humility, righteousness and having absolutely no fear. This spiritual practice grew by leaps and bounds and was a threat to the power structure of the time. Politicians, business and landowners as well as religious leaders needed complete control and obedience of the people to keep their power over the masses. This revolutionary Coptic practice was the biggest threat to the elite, ruling class as those who practiced it became fearless, sovereign beings, which the power structure could not allow to happen. These divine beings were the biggest revolutionary threat to the power structure of this time and they knew it.

In the year 325AD these powerful elites met at a secret meeting called the Council of Nicaea. This is where the rich and powerful made a deal with the Devil. The religious leaders of the time knew they had to lead the masses of people who practiced these mystical rituals down another path. One which led them back into the hands of their corrupt religious leaders. The business and landowners also needed the people to fall back in line so that they could continue to exploit the masses economically by enslaving them with exorbitant rent, frivolous debts and cost of living price gouging. If the people suddenly looked within for their salvation and power, their devious economic plan would be exposed, and the masses would not participate in it. The politicians at this time were also threatened by this revolutionary spiritual practice because it reinforced in the people a direct connection to the Most High, where no human representative was needed to voice their concerns about the power structure or any other affairs that they wanted to address. Every individual's voice carried weight with no fear of speaking out about what is right and exact. Every individual was empowered knowing they were the ones that created their reality and anything that went against their best interests would not be tolerated. They had no fear of death so this could not be used to coerce, bully or manipulate them. This higher level of consciousness left no room for powerful religious leaders, politicians and business owners to have any power or control over the masses.

The elite class came up with a plan straight out of Lucifer's playbook of deception. Instead of individuals finding salvation from within, we will program them to look to us as the authority, outside of themselves in search of their salvation. This will usurp the power from the individual and put it back in the hands of the church and state. We will take out the books of the Bible that empowered the people and encouraged them to seek nothing outside of themselves and replace it with books we will transcribe that fits the ruling class's narrative of needing the church for their salvation. We will rewrite history and change it to our narrative that empowers the ruling class and make the masses weak having low self-esteem and in perpetual self-survival mode to keep them from uniting with one another. We will change the time and dates as we rewrite history leaving them lost and clueless with no way to find themselves in their illustrious past and glorious history. We will replace it with a false narrative, leaving them to think they have been nothing more than savages and heathens throughout time and need the church and state to be civilized and saved. Fear will be their only motivation, and they will believe Love is weak and useless.

This was the downfall of this new African, spiritual practice that was beheaded by the ruling class before it had a chance to grow and thrive. In its place is what you call modern Christianity today. It's just a shadow of what it was intended to be in its organic state. It was originally designed to enlighten and free the masses now it enslaves, oppresses and kills their spirit. Now the people will never have the audacity and courage to die for what they believe is righteous. Now, in the name of this imposter religion called Christianity, it has killed more people in wars under its banner in the history of time. It has enslaved more indigenous people more than any organization in the history of the world. It has collected more money from the poor, downtrodden and the sick. It has sexually abused more victims than we can count. It has given birth to more abusers, serial killers, hypocrites, charlatans, scammers, narcissist, misogynist, racists, pedophiles, sexually deviant and all other demonic behavior than any organization in the history of the world. The Christian cross has been used to decimate entire people, torture non-believers beyond human comprehension, enslave men women and children, rob from the poor and sick and abuse millions of innocent children throughout its history. You tell me is this the religion that transcends a righteous Creator or an organization filled with Lucifer's fallen angels that do his bidding, rewarded handsomely and cowardly hide behind the cross in plain sight.

Present Day Proof That Europeans Still Use the Christian Religion to Manipulate, Exploit and Oppress People of Color

The following Christian based religions were created by white men and women under the auspice of white supremacy to serve their founders at the exploitation of their followers. One must question why the European continues to "reinvent" religion to serve his selfish and egotistical exploits at the expense of it's followers and believers.

RELIGION	EUROPEAN FOUNDER
• Catholicism	Council of Nicaea
• Calvinism	John Calvin
• Church of Latter-Day Saints	Joseph Smith

- **Christian Science Monitor** — **Mary Baker Eddy**
- **Presbyterian** — **John Knox**
- **Amish** — **Jakob Ammann**
- **Quakers** — **George Fox**
- **Methodist** — **John Wesley**
- **Holy Church of God** — **William Phillips**
- **Seventh Day Adventist** — **James Springer**
- **Wicca** — **Gerald Gardner**
- **Scientology** — **L. Ron Hubbard**
- **Church of Satan** — **Anton Lavey**
- **Jehovah Witness** — **Charles Russell**
- **The People's Temple** — **Jim Jones**
- **Branch Davidians** — **David Koresh**
- **Heaven's Gate** — **Marshall Applewhite**
- **Baptist** — **John Smith**
- **Episcopal Church** — **William White**
- **Evangelical Church** — **N/A**
- **Protestant Church** — **Martin Luther**

And many, many, many others!

The number one weapon Lucifer uses to enslave and oppress humanity is religion. That's because its easier to brainwash and condition the multitudes of people by having them believe in doctrine that can be spread to the masses by organized religion. Lucifer controls the one appointed religious leader and the message he conveys to his flock and all the other sheep fall in line to be led to slaughter. It's just that simple. Religion dumbs down and keeps the masses from coming together in unison to revolt against the wealthy and powerful powers that be that rule the world in the shadows. None of your so-called leaders in private practice your religion. They do the opposite of what they brainwash you to believe. You are being programmed to be Non-Player Character

(NPC) in this simulation. A person who lacks original thought, behaves predictably and lacks individuality.

Christianity – 2.4 billion followers

Islam- 1.9 billion followers

Hinduism- 1.2 billion followers

Mind you there is only 8 billion people on the planet!

The Judaism ten commandants imply that God from his higher place of authority "commands" his low life followers to be obedient to him or suffer the consequences. This takes away the power from humans and makes them motivated by the fear of being disobedient and suffering the consequences of their actions. In other words, it relegates humans as being nothing more than childlike and must be scolded and threatened to obey God, because they don't have the ability to self-regulate their morality. On the contrary, the 42 Laws of Maat in ancient Kemet, where the 10 commandments originated from, did not say, God said, "Thou shalt not….." as if humanity was being scolded. They had to recite the 42 Laws before they started their day in the AM and when they ended their day in the PM. They would say to themselves, "I have not….." This was a level of accountability and empowerment that is missing in religion today. It empowered the individual to hold themselves accountable and not a fear-based scolding of a child who was incapable of being righteous and upstanding.

CHAPTER EIGHT
The Devil's Playground

HOLLYWOOD'S EVIL GENIUS

I have always been fascinated by the whole, "going to the movies" experience. At a young age, I was drawn to the theaters and looked upon the experience as a major event in my childhood. Even today, I still cannot attend a movie without a large bucket of popcorn with extra butter and a half-gallon size soft drink, which consists of my own concoction of half fruit punch, preferably Hawaiian Punch and half 7-Up, Sprite or Sierra Mist. On those special occasions I would add the five-pound box of Junior Mints, Kit Kat bar or the 8-pack size of Reese's Peanut Butter Cups. Even though I know these items will eventually kill me, I am still drawn to them like Pavlov's dog, each time I smell that freshly popped popcorn when I first arrive in the movie theater lobby.

This is the exact moment when the brainwashing begins. As soon as one steps inside one of these mega, multiplex movie monstrosities, the moviegoer falls prey to its traps and pitfalls. This is where Hollywood holds its audience hostage in the palm of its hands without them even knowing it. This is where the concept of the "captive audience" originated from. First, Hollywood sets you up in a comfortable, sometimes leather, plush, reclining chair with a cup holder. Then they make sure the theater is nice and cold so that you will pay close attention to the screen and not get too comfortable where they lose your focus and undivided attention. The theater lights are then dimmed so that you will only have the capacity to concentrate on what's on the screen and not be distracted by your immediate surroundings. This forces your undivided attention on the screen in front of you. Next, they pump in surround sound, stereo, THX, HD sound system that has you turning your head every which way, trying to figure out where a particular noise came from. It is very disturbing and embarrassing to look sharply to your right because you thought you heard a baby crying in the seat next to you, only to see a man staring back at you looking for the same source from which the crying sound was coming from. For final measure, they prop this giant 50-foot screen in front of you that acts as a portal to transport the audience from their current reality to an illusion of a reality they force upon their unsuspecting and vulnerable captive audience minds. This is a very powerful tool in mind control. The ability to have an audience see, believe and hear things that do not exist! Do you understand this statement I just made? Hollywood has the capacity and ability to create YOUR reality! Hollywood has the power to control how one perceives not only their environment but how one defines THEMSELVES as well. Hollywood is the master illusionist that uses it audiences as puppets by controlling them with invisible strings.

I continued my passion for cinema when I furthered my education in college. I remember selecting my first elective course, which was entitled Film 101. This course gave me a whole new perspective on how to watch movies and to study film as an art form. I went from "watching movies" to analyzing the intricacies of the art form called, film. I remember the instructor teaching us the underlining themes and images of Orson Wells' classic, cinematic masterpiece, "Citizen Kane." This is where I recognized the story within the story. From that moment on, I looked at all films from a different perspective and maintained a deep passion and appreciation for the message behind the story. From here on out my goal was to not only decipher the plot and theme of a film, but to dissect the spaces in between the plot and theme of the film. I relate this practice similar to observing the raw film on its reel. All film really is a series of images put together and run through a projector at a certain speed to give the illusion of motion, depth, light and substance. I was more focused on the space between the images and not the images themselves. It is in theses "spaces" where the secrets and science of Hollywood were revealed to me. Instead of "reading between the lines" of a book, I was "reading the spaces between the images of a film." This procedure opened a new and unique vantage point and gave me the foundation from which to interpret and decipher movies from here on out.

Besides my passion for cinema, I also carry a passion for Afrikan centered thought, philosophy and culture. This concept also includes traditional, Afrikan spirituality which was the basis for the highest and most advanced civilization known to man. This civilization was known as Kemet, which is located in modern day Egypt. Through my studies of this Afrikan culture, I soon realized the concept of Afrikan spirituality was the foundation for what is known as Metaphysics today. Metaphysics can be broken into two words, Meta and Physics. Meta means after, beyond or adjacent. Physics means the science of matter and energy or the study of nature. Metaphysics is the science of nature beyond or adjacent to matter and energy. It can be described by the following statement. Less than five percent of reality (seen energy) can be deciphered through our five senses of touch, taste, smell, sight or hearing. Ninety-five percent of our reality (unseen energy) cannot be measured or deciphered through these five senses. Metaphysics is the study and recognition of unseen energy through other means besides our five senses. For example, we can see colors, taste foods, hear music, smell fragrances and touch water. These things can be labeled as seen energy. Metaphysics is unseen energy labeled as, invisible energy waves, unseen energy rays, telepathy, "being in the zone," intuition, dreams, spirits, ghosts, angels, spirituality and love. In other words, Metaphysics deciphers the characteristics and properties of unseen energy and how they affect us as living beings. All energy must be accounted for or acknowledged, and their distinctive personalities must be taken into consideration when defining one's reality according to the seen or unseen energies that surround us daily.

My unique view on Hollywood and the film industry may be in direct contrast with the dominant perception today. In my delving into the Afro centric or metaphysical world, I discovered many aspects of science and consciousness that helped me develop a blueprint or key to deciphering Hollywood symbols and images. Hollywood realizes, the best place to hide information from its audiences, is to put it right in front of their faces. Hollywood has made this tactic an elegant art form. I will unveil all my findings to help bring clarity to this unique, sinister and esoteric industry that hypnotizes its victims and makes no apologies for it. Be conscious to the reality or world that has been given to you without you having to say so, in its definition. Consciousness can simply be defined as what an individual pays closest attention to. It is that which we invest our time and energy in focusing on or paying attention to. Consciousness is our unique focal point and interpretation of reality. For example, I may be conscious of the cars zooming by when I am trying to cross a busy street. But I may be unconscious of the tiny creatures, puddles of water and the secret world that dwells under my feet, on the side of the road. So, consciousness has different degrees and levels of participation according to the initiation of the individual. We are all conscious of one thing or another. It is for us to define and interpret for ourselves. Nobody has the right to take that right from us. It is the coercion and invasion of the greatest gift God has given us. The gift of free will or the power to decide and choose for us how we define ourselves and the world we live in. We are all conscious of one thing or another. The trick is to decipher what was forced fed on us and what is innately our personal conclusion in self-actualization. I ask you, the reader, to be conscious of the concepts, philosophy and images that will be revealed in this book. Don't be afraid to put old paradigms aside so you can see things from a different perspective. Cross the threshold into a whole new and different world or reality. Let the cars go by for a second when crossing that same street you have crossed a thousand times before and focus on the world, I am about to reveal to you that was right under your feet this whole time. Be like a child whose mind is open to discovering a reality they never knew existed. I hope it will be as fascinating for you as it was for me. Discover the secret and occult world of Hollywood exposed and the hidden agenda behind their programming.

The Occult History of Holly-Wood

Occult researcher and leading authority on esoteric symbolism, Jordan Maxwell describes the making of Hollywood as such and I paraphrase. "The name Hollywood comes from the ancient mythology of Merlin the Wizard. Merlin used a wand made from Holly wood from the Holly tree. Legend has it that this wood contained magical powers that could be used to cast spells on its unsuspecting victims. This wand would be used by Merlin to manipulate behavior and control anyone who it was used upon." The film industry in "Holly-wood" uses its power, influence and resources to manipulate and control its unsuspecting audiences. "Holly-wood" is used as the primary tool of this elite, secret and select class to keep the masses asleep, disorientated, confused and oblivious to the fact that they are nothing more than sheep that are being led to slaughter by the institutions that enslave them without them even knowing they are slaves. Jordan Maxwell points out other myths of this mysterious Holly wood that was derived by European mythology throughout their history:

- The Celts of the British Isles & Gaul believed the Holly King ruled over death. The Holly King was a warlike giant who bore a great wooden club made of a thick holly branch.

- Japanese legend, Prince Yamato, one of the greatest of the doomed heroes of history & myth, was said to have done battle with a spear the handle of which was made of holly wood, a symbol of divine authority.
- The Yule tree, the Holy Tree ("Holly Tree") (recognized in modern times as the "Christmas tree") is an ancient symbol of life, fertility and vitality.
- Holly is one of the trees said to be the tree of Christ's cross. Legend tells us that the trees of the forests refused the defilement of the cross, splintering into tiny fragments at the touch of the ax. Only the holly behaved like an ordinary tree, allowing itself to be cut and formed into a cross. It is as a Passion symbol that holly is found in pictures of various saints. Its presence indicates that the saint is either reflecting upon Christ's Passion or foretelling it.
- In Germany, holly is called Christdorn in memory of Christ's crown of thorns. According to legend, the holly's branches were woven into a painful crown and placed on Christ's head while the soldiers mocked him saying, "Hail, King of the Jews."
- While many other plants and often weeds (such as Mistletoe) have been deliberately or ignorantly raised up as having ancient significance to our ancestors, no other plant or more universally sacred, more universally mysterious than the Holy Tree, the "Holly".

The Wizard with the magic wand used to cast magical spells on his unsuspecting victims. Notice the modern version of the same Magician using the same hat and "magic" wand made from the mystical holly wood to perform his "Magic."

picsdigger.com/keyword/orchestra%20conductor/

The orchestra conductor also manipulates and controls the musicians playing their instruments (frequencies) by using his wand or holly wood to conduct energy!

According to Jordan Maxwell's research on the mythology of the Holly tree, it has been represented as such.

a. ***A superior warlike weapon, having divine authority.***
b. ***Represents vitality & fertility.***
c. ***Higher consciousness & knowledge.***
d. ***Used to ridicule or mock.***
e. ***Used to crucify or condemn.***
f. ***Maintains mysterious powers.***

These attributes undeniably describe the essence of the film industry. Hollywood is being used as the tool (the wand). This wand is implemented by these elite, secret and occult societies (the wizards). The wizards rule the world to control ("cast a spell") on the unsuspecting masses to further their agenda. All this is being done while the masses stay deaf, dumb and blind to their enslavement.

Furthermore, the actors who portray the characters in Hollywood productions are called the "Cast." They are the ones being used to "cast the spell" on the audiences. The word cast can be defined as; To cause to fall upon something or in a certain direction; send forth: Hollywood also controls television "Broad-Cast." Broad means to cover a wide scope and area. So broadcast is to cast a spell over a wide area. These broadcasts are called television programs. According to Webster's Online Dictionary the word Program means: 1) a brief usually printed outline of the order to be followed, of the features to be presented, and the persons participating (as in a public performance). 2) a plan or system under which action may be taken toward a goal. 3) a plan for the programming of a mechanism (as a computer) b: a sequence of coded instructions that can be inserted into a mechanism (as a computer) c: a sequence of coded instructions (as genes or behavioral responses) that is part of an organism

This definition sheds light on the secret and hidden agenda of Hollywood. According to these formal definitions we are being brainwashed and manipulated by Hollywood programming, broadcasts and movies. Make no mistakes about it. There is a hidden agenda behind every media outlet in America, as well as the world. This book will reveal the concentrated and coordinated effort of the secret power elite behind Hollywood's hidden agenda and programming. This book will expose this hidden, diabolical plot to enslave the masses through esoteric manipulation and control coordinated by a secret society.

In Kemet or what is referred to today as modern day Egypt, our Afrikan ancestors used images and symbols in the form of Metu Neter or what is called hieroglyphics today to communicate with each other and their subconscious minds. There was no written word. Metu Neter when translated literally means God's word. Our ancestors were so advanced that they knew the best form of communication was on the subconscious level. The subconscious level is responsible for controlling over 90% of human behavior. Symbols and images, i.e. Hollywood films speak directly to a person's subconscious mind. This is where we get the saying, "A picture is worth a thousand words." Symbols and images are more powerful than any words that can be spoken. Hollywood uses the power of images and symbols in its film to speak directly to our subconscious in an effort to control and manipulate our behavior, without us ever even knowing it. Remember, all film is a series of images spliced together and run through a projector at a high rate of speed to make it look like the images are animated and alive. This is a very valuable weapon, and this science has been deliberately kept from the masses because of its power, influence and diabolical agenda to enslave the masses.

"The idea that flashing words and images can seep into the subconscious mind and persuade an observer to do something without their awareness came into the public eye in the 1950s. That's when a marketing experiment flashed the message "Drink Coca-Cola" onto a New Jersey movie screen and correlated this to increased Coke sales

in that area. The idea behind the crafty technique: by flickering visuals at a speed greater than your eyes and brain can process or speak at a slightly lower volume than your ears can hear allows messages to sneak past your conscious mind and into your subconscious. The word subliminal derives itself from the Latin word "sub" meaning below and "limen" meaning threshold--below a person's threshold of awareness." --Do Subliminal Messages Really Work?

- By Michelle Bryner

18 March 2010 8:45 AM ET

This is further evidence of Hollywood's secret agenda to program its audience in an elegant method of mind control and brainwashing the masses. Hollywood was founded by wealthy European Jews, but they do not control Hollywood. We are just led to believe that they are in control. They were the first to establish the film industry by usurping Thomas Edison for his patent on the movie projector. Later, they were coerced and strong armed into promoting the agenda of the" Illuminati" or secret ruling class that runs the world in the shadows. These Jewish founders such as Louis B. Mayer, Adolph Zukor, Carl Laemmle, Samuel Goldwyn, William Fox and the Warner brothers were willing to do anything they had to do to keep their lucrative, Hollywood film studios and industries.

The hidden power of elites that also control world governments, unleashed the witch hunt of "McCarthyism" into the film industry about the "so-called" infiltration of Communist in Hollywood. This Communist conspiracy or perceived threat shook the foundation of Hollywood. The Jewish heads of these studios immediately took heed that all that they had built could come tumbling down by means of character assassination and propaganda directly pointed at them, as America's perceived public enemy number one, the Communist. Remember the Jews had the immediate history of persecution by the

Nazis, so they were very fearful and vulnerable to the process of being singled out and ostracized.

In October 1947, several people working in the Hollywood film industry were summoned to appear before the House Committee on Un-American Activities, which had declared its intention to investigate whether Communist agents and sympathizers had been surreptitiously planting propaganda in U.S. films. -- **Schwartz, Richard A. (1999) "How the Film and Television Blacklists Worked". Florida International University. Retrieved 2010-03-03.**

The Motion Picture Alliance for the Preservation of American Ideals (MPA), a political action group cofounded by Walt Disney, issued a pamphlet advising producers on the avoidance of "subtle communistic touches" in their films. Its counsel revolved around a list of ideological prohibitions, such as "Don't smear the free-enterprise system ... Don't smear industrialists ... Don't smear wealth ... Don't smear the profit motive ... Don't deify the 'common man' ... Don't glorify the collective". **--Cohen (2004), pp. 169–70. Forbidden Animation: Censored Cartoons and Blacklisted Animators in America. Jefferson, N.C.: McFarland.**

The HUAC (House of Un-American Activities Committee) hearings had failed to turn up any evidence that Hollywood was secretly disseminating Communist propaganda, but the industry was nonetheless transformed. The fallout from the inquiry was a factor in the decision by Floyd Odlum, the primary owner of RKO Pictures, to get out of the business. As a result, the studio would pass into the hands of Howard Hughes. Within weeks of taking over in May 1948, Hughes fired most of RKO's employees and virtually shut the studio down for half a year as he had the political sympathies of the rest investigated. Then, just as RKO swung back into production, Hughes made the decision to settle a long-standing federal antitrust suit against the industry's Big Five studios. This would be one of the crucial steps in the collapse of the studio system that had governed Hollywood, and ruled much of world cinema, for a quarter-century. - **Lasky, Betty (1989). RKO: The Biggest Little Major of Them All. Santa Monica, California: Roundtable.**

These Jewish, Hollywood moguls were all but willing to do whatever they had to do in an effort to blend in with the American culture to be accepted and at the same time, keep their lucrative, Hollywood empire. With the ruling class secretly pulling the strings and with the support of the U.S. government, these Jewish puppets were more than eager to serve the agenda of their secret and powerful masters. As a consolation prize for serving their masters, these Jews became very wealthy in the process and were allowed to use a percentage of films to promote their Zionist agenda and propaganda as well. There are only six Hollywood film production studios that control which films are made and which ones are not. In order for any film to be made, one must go through one of these studios in order to put out and distribute a film. If they agree to let your film be made, they will be in charge of the overall production of the film. They will have complete control and autonomy of the film. This is why we seem to have the same themes in movies being played over and over again. Hollywood has its own agenda they want to promote. It has nothing to do with the integrity or artistic value of the art of film.

"Hollywood's a place where they'll pay you a thousand dollars for a kiss, and fifty cents for your soul. I know because I turned down the first offer often enough and held out for the fifty cents." - Marilyn Monroe

Movies are an integral part of the fabric of our society. Movies have historically done well for themselves, especially in times of financial hardship or turmoil. During the depression and times of recession, movie profits and attendance always seem to be at their highest. One can relate this phenomenon to the fact that the general population wants to "escape" their own dreary or mundane reality by attending a movie that is going to always have the hero overcome the villain. They relate to the disenfranchised overcoming their hardships. They want to see the good guys always win. They need a hero where one person can defeat all the odds and overcome adversity to achieve their dreams. These images and scenarios are what keep the masses from rebelling. Just like playing the lottery, we all believe we can beat the odds and strike it rich. Sometimes all a person really needs is hope. It's what keeps us getting out of bed every day to go to work at a job that we hate and can't ever seem to get ahead. Hollywood represents the carrot (hope) held in front of the horse (the people) that keeps the cart (the diabolical system) moving forward. We internalize that we are Cinderella. We are Rocky Balboa. We are Bambi. We are Clark Kent. We are Peter Parker. We are Snow White. We are the Lil' Engine That Could. But in reality we are all gullible fools! For every one of us that lives the so-called American Dream, hundreds of thousands are the victims of the American nightmare. We can't all hit the lottery at the same time. There must be millions of losers for the system to function and reward the one winner. But the system only shows us the winner and not the millions of losers who sacrificed everything for a chance to strike it rich. This is how the system flourishes. The illusion that the American Dream can be achieved by "all," is the cruelest and biggest scam America has ever played on the rest of the world and Hollywood serves it up for us to consume on a silver platter.

Tinsel- Something sparkling or showy but basically valueless. Attracting attention to in a vulgar manner. To give a false sparkle to. Superficial. A sham. Shameful or Indecent.

Tinsel Town- A flashy, vulgar tone or atmosphere believed to be characteristic of the American film industry.

"Whoever controls the image and information of the past will determine what and how future generations will think; and, whoever controls the information and images of the present, will also determine how these same people will view the past."
— George Orwell, author of the book

The movie "Focus" starring Will Smith & Margot Harris (2015)

There is a re-released film on Netflix called Focus. It stars Will Smith and Margot Harris, of "Barbie Movie" fame. As you know, Hollywood puts a lot of hidden messages and profound symbolism in their movies, and this movie is no exception. This movie flew under the radar when it came out in 2015. The movie covertly uncovers metaphysical, spiritual and MK Ultra manipulation of the masses. The film is about Will Smith who's a seasoned hustler. He is a master of the art of pickpocketing, manipulation & deception, subtle robberies and an assortment of grifts and scams. Will sees the potential of a "hustle partner" in Margot Harris's character and takes her under his wing as a mentor. He wants to take her under his tutelage to take her scammer game to the next level so they can pull off bigger heists. They met as she was trying to scam him! Will instantly uncovers her nefarious con game and calls her out on it, coincidently he is halfway impressed by her potential. Will then proceeds to secretly follow her and stops her in the middle of the street, while she was walking home. Then and there, Will instructs her on the proper way to pick pocket and demonstrates to her how the game works at the highest level. His deliberate actions directed to her reveal how the masses are manipulated by the subliminal messages, brainwashing, programming and conditioning of the powers that be.

The title of the movie being named, "Focus," accentuates, what humans focus on becomes their reality and what you don't focus on is where your hidden, master Lucifer dwells. The attention of the masses is used to manipulate their behavior and misdirect humans on what not to pay attention to. They get you to look right, while they do something on your left. They have you look up, while they do something below you that goes against your best interest. Will shows Margot how to pickpocket a victim by tapping her on her right shoulder while simultaneously entering her left pocket as her mind can't process two stimulations at the same time. The strong stimuli become the distraction while the subtle stimuli does all the damage. This is also done to humans on a larger scale. They distract you with big headlines while the smaller stories that don't make the news have the biggest impact on you.

Will stands closer to Margot while getting her to look down at his right hand. He proceeds to confide in her that people naturally will focus on people who invade their personal space as a defense mechanism. He then points to a pretend map that he is holding as he knows her gaze will focus on what he is focused on. While she intensely looks at the map as a distraction, his hand goes behind her back and picks her wallet from her purse. He tells her it's all about misdirection. The Devil knows how the human brain operates better than you do and manipulates human nature to take advantage of you while he hides in the shadows!

Will hires Margot for his big score at the Super Bowl once he catches her up to speed on the con. Will knows that next to his luxury super bowl suite he bought, will be a big time, Asian gambler who can't resist any game of chance. Will attends the Super Bowl game and starts making small $1 bets with Margot on little idiosyncrasies that are happening in the football game. He makes sure the Asian gambler is with in an earshot of all the action. As Will and Margot continue to bet and banter with each other, the Asian man can't help but intervene. Once Will's mark is hooked, he proceeds to lose incrementally to the Asian man, as the stakes increase. Will pretends to look dejected and seems more desperate to win his money back from the Asian man. Will eventually falls into a one-million-dollar deficit that he owes the Asian man and desperately tells him he will bet $2,000,000 on their final wager. The Asian man reluctantly agrees as Will appears distraught and desperate. Will tells the Asian man the parameters of the bet. He informs him that Margot, his partner, will pick out a football player's number from the field and if the Asian man randomly picks the same player that Margot secretly wrote down, Will wins the bet and gets the $2,000,000. If the Asian man picks any other number besides the one Margot picked, he wins the bet and the $2,000,000. The Asian man feels he can't lose as there are approximately a total of 200 players on both teams on the field and the odds are heavily in his favor. The Asian man *attentively scans the football field and eventually picks his number with a huge grin on his face knowing its not possible that Margot has picked the same player's number he did. Margot reluctantly tells the Asian man what number she picked and he immediately collapses in disbelief as he has picked the same number, that number being the #55! Will and Margot immediately grab his bag of cash of their winnings and exit the stadium expeditiously, leaving the Asian man bewildered and dumbfounded as he contemplates how they were able to pull this off. Margot excitedly asks Will how he came up with this perceived miracle as she was purposely left out the loop so she would be as natural as possible and make the con more believable.*

Will informs her of his diabolical plan. The week prior to the Super Bowl, Will had marked the Asian man as his next victim researching and knowing all about his gambling addiction, personality traits and idiosyncrasies Will secretly prepped, programmed and conditioned him for the con, a week before the game was to be played. Will knew that he wanted the man to pick the #55 on the field on his final $2,000,000 bet as that was the big payout. Will was going for this bet all along, so he lost on purpose to get to that last two million dollar bet.. He subliminally planted the seed in the Asian man's subconscious mind to coerce and persuade him to pick that number fifty-five when the time of the bet would come a week later during the Super Bowl game.

Will knew the subconscious mind of all humans, only responds or communicates through images and symbols. Will made sure that a week prior to the game the Asian man was bombarded with the symbol of the number fifty-five and was blatantly infiltrated in the man's surroundings and environment wherever he went for that final week. The Asian man was not consciously aware of these subliminal images around him, but his subconscious mind is soaking it up like a sponge unbeknownst to him! Number fifty-five is now imprinted permanently in the man's subconscious mind only to be activated later when the time comes for the big bet. The Asian man doesn't know that he saw this number wherever he went for a week prior, but the #55 is permanently ingrained or branded in his brain. Coincidentally, our subconscious mind is what controls over 90% of our behavior. Humans don't realize that he who controls the images and symbols of their environment control over 90% of their behavior! This is why Super Bowl ads go for millions of dollars for 30 second commercials. Because the work in brainwashing the observers mind into buying their product translates into 100's of millions of dollars from their customers not including "brand loyalty," which means creating a customer for the duration of their lifetime!

Will covertly implanted the symbol of the #55 all around the Asian man's environment. It was in the chandeliers in his hotel room. It was in his hotel room number. On the wallpaper in his hotel hallway. It was on the lapel of the hotel's door man. He hired actors to picket by the hotel with signs that said, "Union 55." It was on taxi cabs, advertisements and billboards surrounding his hotel. They even played a song entitled "Woo Hoo" around him that literally means 5-5 in an Asian language. When it comes time for the big bet on Super Bowl Sunday, our Asian gambler doesn't realize he has no choice but to obey his subconscious mind and pick the player on the football field that is wearing the #55. Thus, Will has already won the bet before he even makes the wager with the Asian gambler a week later!

Just like the Asian gambler in the movie, "Focus," you are also being programmed and brainwashed. You are being conditioned. You are MK Ultra'd. You are being hypnotized in your subconscious mind by images and symbols in your surroundings strategically placed there by your unseen master to control your every move! That's why every news program on every channel or station is on repeat with Lucifer's echo chamber message. Even when you change the channel all the news programs are talking about the same thing because they all are reading off the same scripts on repeat! They all have the same talking points because they are all programming you in controlled opposition like they do in professional wrestling before the big match. What the masses don't realize is that their reality has already been scripted out before it is fed to you. The hero, the villain, the damsel in distress and the heel are all playing roles before you that have already been predetermined. It is a drama scripted out and played in front of you in real time. You are the Mark of the Beast! You are being played in an eloquent song and dance scam that requires your focus to create the reality they want for you! Next time when a thought pops into your head ask yourself. Are you thinking your thoughts or are your thoughts thinking you?

Poly Tricks:

The word "poly" meaning many and "tricks" meaning deceiving the masses into believing they have an active participation or role in what goes on in the government. The "Government:" to Govern the Mental or to keep the masses at a lower level of consciousness and intelligence. Political Science is based on the manipulation of the mechanics and functions of the human brain. Humans have two hemispheres of the brain your right and your left brain. This is why you have the Republican Party which is the "Far Right." Because the "right side" of the human body is controlled by the left hemisphere of the brain. The Democratic Party is "Far Left." The "Left" side of the body is controlled by the right hemisphere of the brain. There are different aspects of these two hemispheres of your brain. The left hemisphere of your brain can only decipher reality through your five senses of what you can see, hear, taste, touch, and smell. Anything outside of your five senses does not exist in the left brain's interpretation of reality. There is no concept of spirituality, compassion, empathy, love or nurturing. The left brain is strictly only interested in obtaining food, shelter, clothing, transportation, avoiding pain and seeking pleasure. Consequently, this is the foundational agenda of the Republican Party. They label themselves Conservative. Conservative meaning all the resources that they acquire are reserved only for their own self-survival. It is not about helping others less fortunate than themselves. Every man is out for themselves as survival of the fittest is the law of the land. They are "conserving" their resources and energy for themselves and any extras goes into their coffers for a rainy day.

The Republican party's mascot is the elephant. The elephant's characteristic is that he does not move for anyone. He is stationary and dares anyone to get in his way. He is "stuck" in his ways and will not budge until he is ready to move. Republicans are the same way and known for their stubbornness and being hardheaded. Republicans also adopt the color red as in the same color as the ancient Vedic root chakra. Remember, the root chakra is only interested in its own self-survival and has no compassion for others. These are also tenets of the conservative, Republican party. All other groups are on their own with no exceptions to the unfortunate circumstances they may find themselves in. Republicans are only for Republicans period and do not apologize for it. These beliefs and faculties contribute to the characteristics of the left hemisphere of the human brain and are needed for survival.

On the other hand, the Democrats, on the "Left" are the opposite of this ideology as they represent the right brain. The characteristic of the right brain is expansive, infinite and inclusive. The right hemisphere of the brain wants to care for everybody regardless of who you are, where you come from, what religious affiliation you are, gender, sex, economic status and so on. Everyone is invited to a right brain party! There are plenty of seats for everybody to be included. If there are no seats they will create more. This is why Democrats are labeled as "Progressive." "Pro" means to place before others and "Gress" means to act. Put these two definitions together and you got, 'those who take action looking out for others." The Democratic Party's mascot is the donkey. The ass or mule is an amalgamation of two animals, so it is "all inclusive" by nature. It is also a work horse, so its nature is to help others at the expense of itself. The official color of the Democratic party is blue which represents the ancient Vedic blue chakra. It is the blue chakra located in the throat that is responsible for communication. This is why Liberals are always willing to listen to everyone's sad story or predicament. They are very empathetic to all causes. They also speak out when others are being mistreated.

Neither the right brain or left-brain characteristics and philosophies are wrong in and of themselves. Humans need both right and left-brain consciousness for humans to function in their totality. There are times humans need to put your individual needs as your priority for self-preservation. Other times when in abundance, humans need to share what they have with others less fortunate. In this way, in times of feast or famine humans can all benefit from each other as you are all connected and isolation is just an illusion. Humanity is a global phenomenon and what affects one human will eventually affect us all. Does Covid 19 and the pandemic ring a bell? The trick politics implements are forcing its participants to choose a side! One is either labeled, a Far Right, Conservative Republican or you are a Far Left, Progressive Democrat. There can be no in between. You must pick a side. You are either with us or against us. You are either part of the problem or part of the solution. Ask anyone in the Trump cult called, MAGA." Thus, by design, no balance or compromise can ever be accomplished by the masses in this Luciferian system. This reassures that the system will inevitably be in place for as long as the country exists and the people will permanently be divided, thus they will never rebel, and they will inevitably take their frustrations out on the "opposite party" and not on the corrupt system Lucifer put into place.

Lucifer's "Polytricks" also steals human's energy, your most precious resource. For your voice to be heard they conditioned you that humans must Vote and this is the only alternative expression to change the system. They say if you don't vote you can't complain. The word, Vote sounds very close to the word "Volt" which is a measurement of energy known as electricity. Like the movie Matrix revealed, Lucifer steals your energy to power the very system that enslaves you. Remember, the Devil can't take your soul, you must give it to him voluntarily. When you give your energy to him it's called voting at the "Polls." A Pole is a conductor of energy that creates a circuit. That's why judges are designated to "Circuits" to usurp your energy when you go to court after being "Charged" with a crime like, "Battery" to eventually put you in a "Cell." Human's vote at an "Election" and your vote is counted by the "Electoral College." This completes the circuit of electricity, otherwise known as, human power, usurped by Lucifer using the Caucasian race to do his bidding. Lucifer created a diabolical system that manipulates human's right and left hemispheres of their brain to enslave them and keep them trapped in Hell without them being aware or conscious of it.

CHAPTER NINE

Set For Life!

What does ancient Kemetic mythology say about similar characters of Lucifer or the Devil in their cultural mythology? As you know ancient Kemet predates Christianity by thousands of years. In the beginning of Kemet, there was a god named Set. Set is the root word where we get the concept of Satan from. Set was depicted as an amalgamation of different animals associated with the dirt and digging underground. Animals such as an Aardvark, Ass, Camel, Mouse and Pig. He was depicted as such because he represented man's lower, animalistic nature. Kemetic gods of higher nature were depicted and associated with birds and had wings as this was associated with transcending and spiritual transformation as they lived in heaven. Thus, the lower the god was to the underground or Hell, the least spiritually evolved their consciousness was. Set was the lowest nature out of all the gods in Kemet. Set represented chaos, storms, death sickness, deceit, unrighteousness, violence, invaders and destabilization. In human consciousness Set represented the human Ego. He was that voice in your head telling you to do wrong when you think no one is watching. Set tells you to quit when you are tired and want to give up. Set tells you to cut corners when you are frustrated. Set uses your self- victimization as an excuse to hurt others or to justify your morally corrupt behavior. Set brags about himself while he demeans others to make himself feel better. Set is selfish and self-absorbed. He only cares about how he is perceived by others but doesn't internalize characteristics such as courage, humility, compassion, integrity, character or selflessness. Set is the raw animalistic nature in man that is driven by ego. This is the origin of the concept of the Christian Satan or the Islamic Shaytan. They originally represented man's lower natured adversary that all humans embody. He is the devil on your shoulder telling you to cut corners, lie, cheat or steal because no one is watching and you won't get caught. Human consciousness is always tempting you and trying to influence your behavior to lower your standards and integrity. The ancients believed that the god Set or man's Ego was in the left hemisphere of the human brain. The left brain is analytical, so it categorizes by putting things in a "box" in order to make sense out of this world. Once a concept goes into one of its boxes, it can never come back out. The left brain does not have the capacity to reevaluate concepts when new information on the contrary to the original belief it discovered. Humans need the malleable right brain to reconfigure ever changing concepts and ideas. Satan uses these characteristics of the left brain to put "You" in a box to imprison you! Those people who are hard-headed and stubborn take their prison with them wherever they go. This is how Satan can enslave you without physically putting shackles on your body. The god Set thrives in a chaotic environment with no order or stability. It is in this atmosphere that corruption thrives in. Without laws and righteous principles to guide man, the ego will take over and lead man down into the depths of Hell in his mind. He will start to think about evil deeds, and they will come into fruition. This is the concept of Babylon, Sodom and Gomorrah and he Roman Empire specifically under Nero. This is what Donald Trump is ushering into the United States. Although the U.S. system is corrupt at its foundation. Donald Trump has now made it fashionable to be lawless and egotistical for the world to see. He is setting the tone for all people of questionable character to come out the hiding and exploit anyone they see fit. Welcome to the "Rise of the Narcissist!"

The Ego must be kept in check or man falls further into chaos and takes his woman and children with him. The ancients knew about the Ego, embodied as the god Set, so they proactively tried to suppress it with righteousness, truth, propriety, reciprocity, humility, honor and selflessness. They used 42 Laws or Principles which they called the goddess Maat to guide them in their everyday lives. Coincidently, this is where the ten commandments originated from. The ancients knew that their egos or the god Set could not be eliminated completely so the best strategy was to try to suppress it by starving it. They did this by having integrity and self-awareness to separate it from your "higher self," which was the consciousness of defining themselves as spiritual beings having a human experience.

Coincidently presently, Lucifer also knows this weakness or flaw in humans. Lucifer does the opposite than our ancient ancestors did. He feeds man's ego constantly. He motivates man thru fear, lack, jealousy, envy, insecurity, vainness, trauma, triggers, lies and deceit, pride, division, chaos, self-survival, pettiness, insecurity and hate. Satan now has humans racing to the bottom of their consciousness and not overcoming their ego to be spiritual beings having a human experience. Humans have fallen so far from their spirituality that they now worship Lucifer without them even knowing it! Humans now look at themselves as human animals that occasionally have spiritual moments. Every time humans wear a designer product or name brand they worship the insecurity in you. Which is Satan's consciousness. Every time humans put processed food in their mouths they are worshipping the devil. Every time humans take a prescription or drug for a disease they can cure if they just change their lifestyle, they are praising Lucifer! Every time humans partake in an addiction to escape or self-medicate they are devil worshippers! This may sound harsh to you but if you realized how far you humans have fallen and have been tricked into living this lower-level existence you would understand. You have been a slave to your ego/ the god Set, your whole life. You do not understand what Love means because you have NEVER experienced it. You are an addict, which is the lowest level of human conscience you can descend to. You are broken and have never seen a glimpse of your true human potential! It was secretly taken away from you at birth thus you never realized or experienced it. You are a shell of what your Creator intended you to be in your natural divine state and you been fooled by an illusion that YOU give credence to that is looking to destroy, subjugate, abuse, manipulate and control you. You are literally a shell of your higher self! You are the walking dead.

Here are some clues to your constant manipulation of Satan I an effort to control your every move. In Kemet, they named the god Set because hid higher consciousness in humans that was concealed and kept man's enlightenment in the dark or unknown altogether. This is where the word, "Sun-Set" came from. The Sun has always represented human's enlightenment, divinity and god consciousness. The" Setting" of the Sun represented man descending into darkness like the "Dark" Ages compared to the Age of "Enlightenment." Presently, words in the English language that contain the name "Set," are directly correlated with keeping humans at their lowest level of animalistic consciousness today.

- **Default Settings**- All electronics and systems are "preprogrammed by Set" before they arrive in your hands. From cell phones, video games, TV's, computers, apps, programs, electronic devices and the like, are all "Pre Set" to a frequency that contributes to the fall and suppression of consciousness in man. All Default Settings are designed to lower human consciousness.
- **To Set-tle**- Whenever we "Settle" we compromise our integrity and give in to Lucifer. When we Settle and lower our standards we worship the Devil. The material that usually "settles" at the bottom

is often the most discarded, least desirable and considered residue or waste.

- **On your mark, Get Set, Go!** – I remember when I was a little boy, we always had foot races in the street to see who was the fastest on our block. This phrase was always how we started the race. Little did we know we were worshipping Satan by saying on your Mark, "Get Set," Go! Set controls the race of life we blindly participate in but can never win.
- **The truth shall Set you free!** – This phrase suggests the dichotomy of truth and falsehood represented by Set. It implies that the falsehood of Set is what is imprisoning humanity. Their only way out is not only knowing the truth but living a righteous life. Knowing and living in Truth is how you free yourself from Set.
- **Set-tle Down**- This phrase seems harmless at first glance. But always know that the god Set is always trying to lower man's consciousness to that of a beast. Set never rises he always tears down to bring you down and keep you in Hell. Set is always pulling things down, never raising things higher. This is why the term "Set Up" has a lower-level connotation of being tricked or fooled. Whereas "Settling Down" is more accepted.
- **The term Settler**- refers to an outside invader who takes over a land that is foreign to him in order to forcefully move the natives out by any means necessary so he can claim the land for his own people to take over.
- **Set in your ways**- Remember stubbornness and being prideful are character traits of the Ego.
- **Quiet on the Set**- The "Set" being referred in this phrase correlates to creating an artificial environment that mimics something real to fool the masses with their television broadcasting a spell and programming.
- **Set In Motion**- To begin to embrace human's animalistic, lower-level behaviors.

- **Set the stage**- To lay the foundation that supports human's animalistic and lower nature.
- **Set eyes on you**- To lust after something which is a lower level, animalistic character trait.
- **Set Apart**- To separate from human's higher nature and embrace the lower animalistic nature in humans.
- **Set Aside**- To separate from human's higher nature and embrace the lower animalistic nature in humans.
- **Set them free**- The act of freeing from man's animalistic lower-level consciousness.
- **Set the table**- Preparing to indulge in gluttony and self-indulgence before humans eat a meal.
- **Dead Set against**- The correlation between man's lower-level consciousness and the concept of death.
- **Game, Set, Match**- The worship and display of man's competitive nature in sports, which embraces ego and human's animalistic nature.
- **Set of twins**- The dual nature of humans having a lower animalistic nature as well as a higher, spiritual consciousness.
- **Heart Set On It** - The heart is where love, humility, selflessness and sacrifice reside. Which is the opposite of Set, who represents the ego. A play on words trick humans into believing that lusting for something somehow correlates to the concept of Love.
- **Jet Setting**- Living a lavish lifestyle of ego, gluttony, wastefulness and false pride. These character traits feed human's ego thus worship the devil.
- **Set Back**- The concept of the god Set always going backwards, always keeping his foot permanently fixed on top of your neck.
- **Set Foot On**- The left foot forward activates the right hemisphere of the human brain where man's higher self-resides. This phrase accentuates that the right foot which activates the ego is man's natural animalistic nature.

- **Set it Off**- Can literally be translated into the god Set of human's ego turning off the path to man's higher self.
- **Set fire or ablaze**- The element of fire is masculine in nature and equivalent to the energy in humans that fuels their animalistic nature and desires.
- **Set out**- To unleash the Ego or man's lower animalistic nature.
- **Set straight**- The path to do wrong in this dimension is easy and plentiful. The road to righteousness is treacherous, dangerous curves and narrow.
- **Set the Bar**- The standard consciousness in this realm is man's lower animalistic nature. This is the standard for all humans.
- **Set Up Shop**- The dominant economic system here is Capitalism. Which can be defined as capitalizing on human's weakness, desperations, kindness, gullibility and insecurities to exploit money out of them.
- **Set Sail**- The element of water contains feminine traits related to higher consciousness. The phrase suggests that Set dominates this consciousness by navigating on top of it to show its mastery over it.

Doctors describe how the Ego/Set tricks Humanity.

"The ego/Set is the worst confidence trickster we could ever figure, we could ever imagine. Cause you don't see it. – Dr. Yoav Dattilo, Ph. D

"And the single biggest con is "I am you."
– Dr. Steven C. Hayes Ph. D

"The problem is that the ego/Set hides in the last place you will ever look—within itself." – Dr. Peter Fonagy, Ph. D

"It disguises its thoughts as your thoughts its feelings as your feelings. You think it's you." – Leonard Jacobson

"Peoples' need to protect their own ego/Set knows no bounds. They will lie, cheat, steal and kill and do whatever it takes to maintain what we call ego boundaries." – Andrew Samuels, Ph. D

"People have no clue that they're imprisoned. They don't know that there is an ego/Set. They don't know the distinction." - Leonard Jacobson

"At first it is difficult for the mind to accept that there is something beyond itself, that there's something of greater value and greater capacity discerning truth then itself." – Dr. David Hawkins, M.D. Ph. D

"In religion, the Ego manifests itself as the devil. And of course, no one realizes how smart the Ego is because it created the devil so you can blame somebody else. – Dr. Deepak Chopra, M.D.

"In creating this imaginary external enemy, it usually made a real enemy for ourselves, and that becomes a real danger to the ego/Set, but that's also the ego's creation."- Dr. Peter Fonagy, PhD.

"There is no such thing as an external enemy, no matter what that voice in your head is telling you. All perception of an enemy is a projection of the ego/Set as the enemy."- Dr. Deepak Chopra, M.D.

"In that sense, you can say 100% of our external enemies are of our own creation." – Dr. Fonagy, PhD.

"Your greatest enemy is your own perception, is your own ignorance, it is your own ego/Set." - Dr. Obadiah S. Harris, PhD.

The collection of quotes I've shared touch on a central theme in psychology, philosophy, and spirituality: the concept of the "ego" and its role in shaping our perception, behavior, and relationship with ourselves and the world around us.

The ego, in psychological terms, is often referred to as our conscious self or the aspect of our personality that we consider "us." It's responsible for our thoughts, feelings, and actions, and it mediates between our basic desires (the id, in Freudian terms) and the moral and societal expectations we internalize (the superego). The ego is essentially our sense of identity.

However, many of the quotes I've shared adopt a more spiritual or philosophical perspective on the ego, painting it as an entity that can mislead or imprison us, that can cause us to perceive external enemies, and that can push us to destructive behaviors in the name of protecting itself.

Here's a brief breakdown of some of the ideas mentioned in these quotes:

1. **Ego as a deceptive force:** Many of the quotes imply that the ego can deceive us into thinking its thoughts and feelings are our true, authentic selves. This echoes the view of the ego as a false self or a constructed persona that hides our true nature. It is the Devil that resides in our psyche. That negative voice in our heads we can never get rid of.
2. **Ego as a source of conflict:** The ego creates external enemies as a means of reinforcing its own identity and deflecting responsibility for internal conflicts. This can lead to a cycle of blame and hostility, further distancing us from understanding our true selves and potential. The Devil never apologizes. It is never wrong.
3. **Ego as a barrier to self-realization:** The idea that the ego can prevent us from recognizing a reality beyond itself is a common theme in spiritual and philosophical traditions. Overcoming or transcending the ego is often seen as a path to enlightenment, self-

realization, or a deeper understanding of the universe. Ego traps you in Hell.

4. **Ego as self-created enemy:** This concept underscores the idea that our perceptions of external threats or enemies are often projections of our own fears, insecurities, and unresolved internal conflicts. Hell is a state of mind that was created by our conditioning and programming.

These perspectives on the ego can help us understand the ways in which our perceived identity can distort our perspective and limit our potential. By acknowledging and exploring the role of the ego, we can work towards greater self-awareness, empathy, and understanding, both in our relationships with others and with ourselves.

Lastly, another clue that this physical realm is Hell controlled by Lucifer can be found in the blueprint of the criminal justice system. Being in the industry, I discovered one fact that all criminals have in common and that is this. **ALL CRIMES COMMITTED BY HUMANS ARE COMMITTED BY THEIR EGOS!** But there is not one program in the criminal justice system that addresses the concept of the human ego. If humans can separate themselves from their egos, there would be no need for jails or prisons. This is a telling fact that the system is not looking to rehabilitate criminals but make more money off their slave labor and disingenuous programs that continue the vicious cycle of criminality. Not only does the ego commit every crime that's ever been committed, it also creates victims. The same energy that you will have violate, abuse and traumatize a person on the victim's side they feel guilty that it was done to them. They're not apt to tell people that they're in an abusive relationship for fear what other people will think about them. That's also ego. The pride before the fall. The victim would rather suffer in silence, then suffer an ego death and let people know that they have been a fool by being victimized for a long period of time. This is why victims don't leave abusive relationships. That's why they don't seek help. The ego tells you it's worse what people will say or think about you then it would be to reveal what is happening to you and leave an unhealthy situation.

"He will murder his brother to possess his brother's land. Let him not breed in great numbers, for he will make a desert of his home and yours. Shun him; drive him back into his jungle lair, for he is the harbinger of death. "The Lawgiver," (as spoken by Cornelius in Planet of the Apes)

For people of color in general and Black people in particular, this paradigm shift in this physical realm has targeted them as a means of exploitation in sustaining this corrupt global system that serves your initiated, white masters. Since the fall of ancient, melanated civilizations around the globe, an elite convention of people who classify themselves as white, have targeted them, their resources, their knowledge and more importantly their spiritual power as a means to not only suppress their God given powers but also to support and fuel this world they have built for themselves at their expense. This shift was made around 2000 years ago beginning in the Age of Pisces. This was done by elaborate design. The consciousness of this Age is the motto, "I believe." This consciousness keeps the masses asleep and herded as sheep or schools of fish, with no minds of their own. People of color were being groomed as followers who never questioned authority. Coincidently, this is the first year of our lord and the establishment of Christianity as the authority of the world's power base. Christianity made people of color's image of God from looking like them to having European features of white skin, blue eyes and stringy blonde hair. I.e. the figure Jesus Christ. This was done by design. It was intentionally the opposite phenotype of who the indigenous identified themselves as. As a result, this automatically created a psyche of self-hate which perpetually shut down people of color's spiritual consciousness and implemented a culture of self-sabotage and low self-esteem. These actions caused ridicule, betrayal and shame throughout their communities which led to their downfall and vulnerability. This led to the exploitation and manipulation by their white masters to gain favor with them. If a group of indigenous people hate themselves, you will no longer need to destroy them as they will gladly and unconsciously do it to themselves. One just has to be patient and let this cancerous consciousness infect and devastate the indigenous community leaving it vulnerable for exploitation and manipulation from outside invaders, who looked like their new found god, Jesus Christ. For good measure, they also erased and "reset" time and made this Year One AD with the ushering in of this brainwashing and mind control psyops, otherwise known as, Christianity. This act implied that all the ancient melanated, advanced civilizations, history, sciences, philosophies, cultures and technologies will be lost and forgotten. These diabolical implementations were intentionally set in place so the white power structure, using Christianity at its base, can rule with an iron fist, using the system of white supremacy, for the next two thousand years and never be challenged by the unsuspecting indigenous masses that are under the conscience spell of, "I Believe," without ever questioning authority for the next 2,000 years. As the Age of Pisces is ending the spell of "I Believe" consciousness is wearing thin. The white power structure had to do something drastic and traumatic to keep Black people under their spell for another 2,000 years. You see the next Age that follows Pisces is the Age of Aquarius. This is the Age of "I Know." As you can see, going from the consciousness of "believing" everything that you are told to "knowing" when to question authority that doesn't make sense can be very dangerous to the oppressor if the oppressed starts to awaken and starts to have discernment. Chattel slavery is introduced through the Middle Passage. With the consent of the Catholic church, which is the head of Christianity. European countries started invading Africa to rape, pillage and plunder her natural resources which included the African people. One by one European countries such as Spain,

Portugal, Italy, Belgium, Germany, England, France, Greece and many others descended on Africa like locusts to devour all her resources and oppress the African people. The enslaved Africans were then taken on ships across the Diaspora to countries like Brazil, Venezuela, Columbia, Panama, Cuba, Jamaica, Trinidad, Belize, Costa Rica, Haiti, Dominican Republic and the Americas to work on plantations until they died. Shortly thereafter, in the Americas, they found it was cheaper to breed the enslaved indigenous people in their colonies rather than import them from Africa. It was the United States that thrived and mastered this diabolical procedure called breeding camps to make a man, woman and child bow down and be subservient to your will from the womb to the grave. Hence the Nigger is born! Taken from the art of horse breeding, torture as a means of control, sexual trauma and deep psychological manipulation, the finest specimens the Black race has to offer unknowingly led other indigenous races from around the world to the bottom of spiritual awareness and lower-level consciousness. The Age of Aquarius, "I Know" consciousness is now replaced by the "Nigger Mentality" consciousness that permeates the sons and daughters of enslaved indigenous people around the world. You see, so-called Black Americans lead the world in most categories when it comes to cultural identities. Black Americans influence the world in, Spirituality, Sports, Entertainment, Language, Music, Fashion, Dance, Art and culture. As the Black American goes, other indigenous people from around the world will follow. You control the consciousness of the Black American man, woman and child and you control the consciousness of all people of color throughout the diaspora. Let's dive deeper into how a once proud, indigenous, royal family gets torn apart for 500 years to keep them from achieving higher levels of consciousness which would free all indigenous people around the world.

The Wille Lynch Letter Excerpts: Willie Lynch – The making of a slave – Virginia USA 1712

This speech was delivered by Willie Lynch on the bank of the James River in the colony of Virginia in 1712. Lynch was a British slave owner in the West Indies. He was invited to the colony of Virginia in 1712 to teach his methods to slave owners there. The term "lynching" is derived from his last name. LET'S MAKE A BLACK MAN A SLAVE! "Gentlemen, you know what your problems are; I do not need to elaborate. I am not here to enumerate your problems; I am here to introduce you to a method of solving them. In my bag here, I HAVE A FULL PROOF METHOD FOR CONTROLLING YOUR BLACK SLAVES. I guarantee every one of you that if installed correctly IT WILL CONTROL THE SLAVES FOR AT LEAST 300 HUNDREDS OF YEARS. My method is simple. Any member of your family or your overseer can use it. I HAVE OUTLINED A NUMBER OF DIFFERENCES AMONG THE SLAVES; AND I TAKE THESE DIFFERENCES AND MAKE THEM BIGGER. I USE FEAR, DISTRUST AND ENVY FOR CONTROL PURPOSES. These methods have worked on my modest plantation in the West Indies, and it will work throughout the South. Take this simple little list of differences and think about them. On top of my list is "AGE" but it's there only because it starts with an "A." The second is "COLOR" or shade, there is INTELLIGENCE, SIZE, SEX, SIZES OF PLANTATIONS, STATUS on plantations, ATTITUDE of owners, whether the slaves live in the valley, on a hill, East, West, North, South, have fine hair, course hair, or is tall or short. Now that you have a list of differences, I shall give you an outline of action, but before that, I shall assure you that DISTRUST IS STRONGER THAN TRUST AND ENVY STRONGER THAN ADULATION, RESPECT OR ADMIRATION. The Black slaves after receiving this indoctrination, shall carry on and will become self-refueling and self-generating for HUNDREDS of years, maybe THOUSANDS. Don't forget you must pitch the OLD black Male vs. the YOUNG black Male, and the YOUNG black Male against the OLD black male. You must use the DARK skin slaves vs. the LIGHT skin slaves, and the LIGHT skin slaves vs. the DARK skin slaves. You must use the FEMALE vs. the MALE. And the MALE vs. the FEMALE. You must also have your white servants and overseers distrust all Blacks. But it is NECESSARY THAT YOUR SLAVES TRUST AND DEPEND ON US. THEY MUST LOVE, RESPECT AND TRUST ONLY US. Gentlemen, these kits are your keys to control. Use them. Have your wives and children use them, never miss an opportunity. IF USED INTENSELY FOR ONE YEAR, THE SLAVES THEMSELVES WILL REMAIN PERPETUALLY DISTRUSTFUL. Thank you, gentlemen." "For fear that our future Generations may not understand the principles of breaking both beast together, the nigger and the horse. We understand that short range planning economics results in periodic economic chaos; so to avoid turmoil in the economy, it requires us to have breadth and depth in long range comprehensive planning, articulating both skill sharp perceptions. We lay down the following principles for long-term comprehensive economic planning. Both horse and niggers is no good to the economy in the wild or natural state. Both must be BROKEN and TIED together for orderly production. For an orderly future, special and particular attention must be paid to the FEMALE and the YOUNGEST offspring. Both must be CROSSBRED to produce a variety and division of labor. Both must be taught to respond to a peculiar new LANGUAGE. Psychological and physical instruction of CONTAINMENT must be created for both. We hold the six cardinal principles as truth to be self-evident, based upon the following discourse concerning the economics of breaking and tying the horse and the nigger together, all inclusive of the six principles laid down about. NOTE: Neither principle alone will suffice for good economics. All principles must be employed for the orderly good of the nation. Accordingly, both a wild horse and a wild or natural nigger is dangerous even if captured, for they will have the tendency to seek their customary freedom, and in doing so, might kill you in your sleep. You cannot rest. They sleep while you are awake and are awake while you are asleep. They are DANGEROUS near the family house, and it requires too much labor to watch them away from the house. Above all, you cannot get them to work in this natural state. Hence both the horse and the nigger must be broken; that is breaking them from one form of mental life to another. KEEP THE BODY TAKE THE MIND! In other words, break the will to resist. Now the breaking process is the same for both the horse and the nigger, only slightly varying in degrees. But as we said before, there is an art in long range economic planning. YOU MUST KEEP YOUR EYE AND THOUGHTS ON THE FEMALE and the OFFSPRING of the horse and the nigger. A brief discourse in offspring development will shed light on the key to sound economic principles. Pay little attention to the generation of original breaking but CONCENTRATE ON FUTURE GENERATION. Therefore, if you break the FEMALE mother, she will BREAK the offspring in its early years of development and when the offspring is old enough to work, she will deliver it up to you, for her normal female protective tendencies will have been lost in the original breaking process. For example, take the case of the wild stud horse, a female horse and an already infant horse and compare the breaking process with two captured nigger males in their natural state, a pregnant nigger woman with her nigger infant offspring. Take the stud horse, break him for limited containment. Completely break the female horse until she becomes very gentle, whereas you or anybody can ride her in her comfort. Breed the mare and the stud until you have the desired offspring. Then you can turn the stud to freedom until you need him again. Train the female horse whereby she will eat out of your hand, and she will in turn train the infant horse to eat out of your hand also. When it comes to breaking the uncivilized nigger, use the same process, but vary the degree and step up the pressure, to do a complete reversal of the mind. Take the meanest and most restless nigger, strip him of his clothes in front of the remaining male niggers, the female, and the nigger infant, tar and feather him, tie each leg to a different horse faced in opposite directions, set him afire and beat both horses to pull him apart in front of the remaining nigger. The next step is to take a bull whip and beat the remaining nigger male to the point of death, in front of the female and the infant. Don't kill him, but PUT THE FEAR OF GOD IN HIM, for he can be useful for future breeding." THE BREAKING PROCESS OF THE BLACK WOMAN "Take the female and run a series of tests on her to see if she will submit to your desires willingly. Test her in every way, because she is the most important factor for good economics. If she shows any sign of resistance in submitting completely to your will, do not hesitate to use the bull whip on her to extract that last bit of nigger bitch out of her. Take care not to kill her, for in doing so, you spoil a good economy. When in complete submission, she will train her offspring in the early years to submit to labor when they become of age. Understanding is the best thing. Therefore, we shall go deeper into this area of the subject matter concerning what we have produced here in this breaking process of the female nigger. We have reversed the relationship in her natural uncivilized state: she would have a strong dependency on the uncivilized nigger male, and she would have a limited protective tendency toward her independent male offspring and would raise male offspring to be dependent like her. Nature had provided for this type of balance. We reversed nature by burning and pulling a civilized nigger apart and bull whipping the other to the point of death, all in her presence. By her being left alone, unprotected, with the MALE IMAGE DESTROYED, the ordeal caused her to move from her psychological dependent state to a frozen independent state. In this frozen psychological state of independence, she will raise her MALE and female offspring in reversed roles. For fear of the young man's life she will psychologically train him to be MENTALLY WEAK and DEPENDENT, but PHYSICALLY STRONG. Because she has become psychologically independent, she will train her FEMALE offspring to be psychological independent. What have you got? You've got the NIGGER WOMAN OUT FRONT AND THE NIGGER MAN BEHIND AND SCARED. This is a perfect situation of sound sleep and economy.

Before the breaking process, we had to be alertly on guard at all times. Now we can sleep soundly, for out of frozen fear his woman stands guard for us. He cannot get past her early slave molding process. He is a good tool, now ready to be tied to the horse at a tender age. By the time a nigger boy reaches the age of sixteen, he is soundly broken in and ready for a long life of sound and efficient work and the reproduction of a unit of good labor force. Continually through the breaking of uncivilized savage nigger, by throwing the nigger female savage into a frozen psychological state of independence, by killing of the protective male image, and by creating a submissive dependent mind of the nigger male slave, we have created an orbiting cycle that turns on its own axis forever, unless a phenomenon occurs and re shifts the position of the male and female slaves. We show what we mean by example. Take the case of the two economic slave units and examine them closely." THE NEGRO MARRIAGE UNIT "We breed two nigger males with two nigger females. Then we take the nigger male away from them and keep them moving and working. Say one nigger female bears a nigger female and the other bears a nigger male. Both nigger females being without influence of the nigger male image, frozen with a independent psychology, will raise their offspring into reverse positions. The one with the female offspring will teach her to be like herself, independent and negotiable (we negotiate with her, through her, by her, negotiate with her at will). The one with the nigger male offspring, her frozen subconscious fear for his life, will raise him to be mentally dependent and weak, but physically strong, in other words, body over mind. Now in a few years when these two offspring become fertile for early reproduction we will mate and breed them and continue the cycle. That is good, sound, and long range comprehensive planning." —-**Willie Lynch – The making of a slave – Virginia USA 1712**

You may assume the effects of the brutal implementation of this diabolical plan over 150 years ago does not influence Black people in America today and you would be sadly mistaken. A tall tale sign that the results of this plan are going strong today as the day they were first forced upon them is the fact that Black people in America still predominantly define and refer to themselves as Niggers but with an (a). The toxic word Nigger(a) is now spread across the Diaspora as indigenous people around the world define themselves with that vulgar word increasingly each day! If Black people continue to label, define and embrace that word as if they created it for themselves, they will never be free by reaching higher levels of spiritual consciousness. They will be subconsciously trapped in a loop of lower-level consciousness of self-hate that they will continue to perpetuate for generations after generations to come. They will continue to be a race of the "Walking Spiritual Dead" under their white slave master's control. Here is how this "Nigger Mentality" consciousness is subtly administered today and has the same power as it did 500 years ago. Continuation of the Nigger Male Conditioning: For the nigger male child, I would make sure he's born into a system that fears his power before he even knows he has it, and from the moment he takes his first breath, I begin the war, with violence, with shame, not with chains but conditioning. I programmed his nigger parents before he has arrived. Make sure his nigger father is numb, unavailable or absent. Make sure his nigger mother is overwhelmed, unsupported, and uncaring. He enters a home where love is unstable. Safety is conditional, and emotions are never fully seen. That's his blueprint. Then I'd weaponize school. I'd sit him in a chair for six hours a day and punish him for needing to move, explore, or question. I'd make sure his creativeness and restlessness is labeled disorder. I drug his nigger spirit before it grows teeth, and I make sure no one ever tells him he's not broken. This is just normal. I'd confuse his masculinity early. Tell him real nigger men are aggressive, competitive, emotionally shut off. Tell him kindness is weakness. Tell him silence is strength, then I'd mock him when he becomes emotionally unavailable and call him toxic when he cracks. Now, he's confused, ashamed, and disconnected from his core. I fractured his sexuality before he even knew what it is. Normalizing his molestation and sexual abuse forced him. Introduce porn before connection, pleasure before intimacy control before vulnerability. Now, he learns to chase validation through conquest, not love. He'll have sex without ever touching intimately and softly. I tell him his worth is tied to performance, grades, muscles, money, status. Every achievement praised, every emotion ignored. Now, he's addicted to results terrified of failure and ashamed of softness. But no one sees it because he looks successful. I'd isolate him. Make sure he's surrounded by nigger boys, but never truly know strong men. Teach him to joke through pain, distract through humor, and lie with confidence. He'll be the strongest in the room and still feel like a fraud. I keep him in silent competition with every other nigger man. Convince him that brotherhood is a weakness. That vulnerability will get him betrayed. That trusting another nigger man will make him prey. Now, he stands alone, strong, admired, and completely disconnected. I'd wound his heart and make him hide it. Let his first love break him wide open, then tell him to man up. Never speak of it again. Now, every nigger woman he loves after that is filtered through a wound he was never allowed to heal. I keep him chasing something he could never reach: the perfect body, the perfect career, the perfect partner, the perfect moment where he finally feels enough, but it never arrives. The void wasn't created by lack of achievement; it was created by lack of remembrance of his culture. I'd make sure he dies respected, admired, and unknown. The good niggerman that selfishly lived by his ego motivated by fear and avoiding pain and accountability. The one who never asked for help. He'll leave behind a legacy of other broken niggers but take his truth to the Grave. That's how you fracture a nigger man today. Not with erosion but with silence with lies dressed as love until he forgets what it ever felt like to ever want to be whole. Continuation of the Nigger Female Conditioning: I want to fracture the nigger woman from the moment she was born until the moment she died. I'd make her doubt her own body from the very beginning. I tell her she's too much or not enough, too loud, too quiet, too big, too small.

I disconnected her from the rhythm of her womb before she ever did. I would make her ashamed of her cycle and teach her that pain and trauma are normal. That intuition is from the devil. That sensitivity is a weakness. I divide her from her nigger mother, not always through conflict, sometimes through silence. I make sure her nigger mother carries unspoken trauma, passed through tone and tension, not words. So, the nigger daughter grows up confused decoding emotions instead of expressing them. Learning love means scamming, deceiving, fixing and pleasing others at the expense of herself. I'd glamorize beauty and weaponize comparison to beauty standards she can ever achieve. Flood her with images of European perfection. She'll never reach it because the standard of beauty is a white woman with European features that are the opposite of hers. I'd make her chase external validation while starving her internal, knowing now she's too busy hating her reflection to notice. She was born dysfunction. I'd fracture her friendships early, whisper insecurity into the space between. Make her nigger girlfriends compete for attention, affection and approval. Make trust feel dangerous, and betrayal feel inevitable. She will grow into a nigger woman who smiles at other nigger women while bracing for the impact from their betrayal. . I'd confuse her sexuality before she understands what consent means. I will let her experience sexual exploitation before security and love. Let her feel desired before she knows self-respect. Make her believe her worth lies in her desirability, but shame her for expressing her sexuality. Now, she's trapped in a loop, repressing it, expressing it and regretting it. I make her serve those who are not worthy for her to feel loved. Make her a helper, a healer who mothers everyone but herself. Her nigger mother taught her that saying no is selfish and disrespectful. Taking time for herself is an act of selfishness and laziness. Boundaries are rejection, so she gives until she burns out and no one notices. She sells her freedom wrapped in an illusion of feminism. Tell her her power means becoming like a man. Hustle, hardness and selfishness mean success and validation. Suppress the very thing that makes her magic.

Softness, her flow, her intuition, her nurturing, her spiritual wisdom. Convince her to cut off her cultural roots and sacred femininity in the name of reaching financial success. Let her taste what she thinks is love, then take it away from her again, so she starts to believe the problem is her. Now, she shape-shifts, self-abandons, people please, performs just to be chosen. But even when she's chosen, she won't feel safe because she never knew her whole and healed self. Silence is her rage, telling her to be nice, be agreeable, and be quiet that by the time she realizes what's been done to her, it's useless for her to scream. Fill her womb with emotion and rage she was never allowed to express. Generations of grief, guilt and shame consume her. She'll feel the weight, but not the source. She'll think she's broken when, in truth, she's carrying an entire dysfunctional bloodline and unspoken pain. And when she finally starts to wake up and she begins to remember her power, surround her with Christian, religious dogma filled with soft words, safe rituals and surface healing. Let her feel like she's evolving without ever reclaiming her cultural essence. If she truly remembered. If she loved without shame, loved without losing herself and claimed her voice without apology, she'd tear the entire system down just by existing. That's what her enemy fears the most. Not her beauty, not her accomplishments, not her physical strength. They fear that she remembers she is a powerful spiritual, divine being who has no knowledge of herself!

Lyrics of Redemption Song by Bob Marley & The Wailers

"Old pirates, yes, they rob I. Sold I to the merchant ships. Minutes after they took I. From the bottomless pit. But my hand was made strong. By the hand of the Almighty. We forward in this generation Triumphantly, Won't you help to sing. These songs of freedom?

'Cause all I ever have......... Redemption songs."

CHAPTER TEN

Casting Spells & Cursive Writing

Lucifer's fallen angels, aka The Illuminati, created the English language so humans can "Anguish." Remember, the word Grammar comes from the word Grimoire, which means, "Book of Spells!" The Bible tells us, "In the beginning God said let there be Light and there it was." Coincidently, Lucifer the Fallen Angel is known as the "Light Bearer." Is this scripture in the Bible a clue to God creating this physical realm for Lucifer to have domain over?!? God's first command in his creation of the physical dimension was to speak into existence, light otherwise known as, the Electro-Magnetic Spectrum that contains less than 1% of all energy in this realm. Words have the capacity to create "worlds." It just so happens that humans and your limited five senses can only detect this miniscule slither of energy which you call your reality in totality. Humans are oblivious and blinded to the 99% of energy in this realm. This is where Lucifer lurks in the shadows to control and manipulate you. This is where he hides beyond the limits of your five senses. This is where he plays humans like his puppet! This let there be light Bible verse also emphasizes the power in the spoken word. This word was created with the word so it makes sense that Lucifer would manipulate human's language to secretly control and confuse them. This is the genesis of the term "legalese." This is where the Native Americans refer to the white man as speaking with a "Forked Tongue." This is why the "Pen is mightier than the sword." This is where the term "Pencil Whipped" comes from. Remember the two characteristics of the Devil. 1) He cannot forcefully take a human's soul you have to voluntarily give it to him. 2) The greatest trick Lucifer has pulled on humanity is have you believe he does not exist. With these two-character traits in mind, it becomes crystal clear that the biggest scam Lucifer can execute on humanity is the manipulation of the English language to trick humans into creating and sustaining their hellish prison by constantly speaking it into existence.

For example, what is the first thing humans say to themselves when they wake up in the A.M.? Answer: Good Morning. The act of mourning is one of the lowest frequencies humans can adopt as it blocks you from your heart and convinces you that you are a victim with fear, guilt, shame, regret and sorrow. This word sets the tone for the rest of your day to be self-sabotaged as a victim without you even knowing it!

Here is a list of words we use every day that keep us trapped in Hell with no escape in sight.

- **Hello**: Meaning Hell is Low. Subconsciously acknowledging humanities lower-level consciousness or pronounced backwards is Oh Hell!
- **Job:** In the Bible meaning someone who is persecuted beyond measure by Satan.
- **Work Weak:** Implying that working a job you hate just to pay your bills makes humans weak.
- **Weak End**: By the end of your five-day workweek leave you Weakened on your weekends.
- **Weak Daze**: Working at a job you don't like during the weekdays leaves you in a Weak Daze.

- **Awake**: When you wake up to start your work weak is equivalent to going to A Wake, which is a party for the dead at a funeral.
- **Earn/Urn**: At your Job or place of persecution you Urn or Earn a living, which is a container that holds the ashes of the dead.
- **Pay Attention**: Lucifer demands your full attention that you pay everyday with your life.
- **Understand**: Implies that a human's geographical location is "Standing Under" a place of lower frequencies called, Hell.
- **Cursive Spelling or Writing:** The act of writing a curse to keep the spell alive that keeps humans trapped in Hell.
- **Life Sentence:** Spells used in our everyday vernacular and writings, that keeps us cursed in Hell.
- **Undertakings:** Any activity humans engage in that keeps you at a lower level of consciousness. An "Undertaker" takes care of the dead at the cemetery.
- **Trance-Late or Translate:** English language, "Trance" interpretation hypnotizes you into a sleeplike trance that resembles the walking dead. The word "Late" refers to someone who is deceased.

"At first I suspected the hands of collusion entangling the language to foster illusion and I think it's quite true that a culture's theology has a great deal to do with a word's etymology. And how it evolves over time to combine incompatible meanings that may undermine the original thoughts it was to define. But, now I don't think its planned for the thing that I found is that like concepts can gravitate toward the same sound and vibrate at the rate that our thoughts designate. Because words are electro-magnetic vibrations whose fine alphabetic tin tabulations can take on the tint of our true expectations which they then imprint on our mental of mind. Causing sounds to adhere when they are of the same kind. " -Laura Airica

Zombies or the "Walking Dead" refers to the masses of humans who are living unfulfilled lives and a mundane existence.

- Zombies move at a slow and low frequency symbolizing a spiritual death but are still technically alive.
- Zombies can't come out in sunlight they must stay in the dark symbolizing ignorance and unwillingness to acknowledge or raise their lower-level states of mind.
- Zombies find comfort in those around them that have the same lower-level vibration as they are. Misery loves company so they gather, commune and move as one.
- Zombies practice cannibalism as they prey, kill and feast on the weaker Zombies in their group and the people who have higher levels of consciousness they despise.
- Zombie's limbs seem to fall off prematurely symbolizing their unhealthy lifestyle and the inability to take the appropriate action and change their behavior. In other words, they cant save themselves from their own selves.
- Zombies can't speak for "language spells" have already done its toll on them. They have been cursed so language is no longer needed to enslave them.
- Zombies have an insatiable appetite and are motivated by quenching it by any means necessary. They are addicts and define themselves by this animalistic consciousness of satisfying their passion and addictions without a moral compass to guide them.
- Zombies have a lack of empathy for others and are incapable of using reason or logic. If you go against the group, you either get consumed by them or are ostracized from their cult.
- Zombie's motivation for existence is to infect as many people as they can with their lower-level consciousness which acts as a virus, to make themselves feel better.
- Zombies have no discernment or the ability to suppress inappropriate responses of aggression when restraint is called for.

They have no discipline and are motivated by lower-level emotions exclusively.

I have just described "Zombie Behavior" that most humans would consider to be normal functions today. This is "Nigger Mentality" that has been normalized in the Black community.

A.I. Artificial Intelligence is knowledge without the guidance of the heart.

Let's get into Artificial Intelligence and break down how it comes into play in keeping humans programmed to embrace their lower selves, otherwise known as the Ego, so they will be eternally trapped in Hell. As we covered earlier in this chapter, social media platforms diabolically collect 5,000 points of data based on your profile, demographics and search history on their platforms. They gather your personal information on you based on all the data gathered through your time online. This creates a "cyber you" that is forced fed advertisements and data based on your psychological profile it has created from this information that has been gathered by secretly spying on you when you log in. Not only is your information on your profile bought and sold like a "Cyber Slave Auction," to multinational corporations that want to manipulate you into buying their products, but this data is also used to trap you in a box they created for you based on your scrolling history and like and dislikes. This Artificial Identification of you or the "Cyber You," cannot get out of the box or prison that Artificial Intelligence has created for it. In other words, you are not allowed to change your mind about your current views on health, politics, entertainment, education, intelligence, sports, hobbies, etc..... This A.I. entrapment becomes a self-fulling prophecy. Instead of you telling Artificial Intelligence your likes and dislikes, it starts to tell you what you like and dislike. It will only feed and show you information online based on the original profile it imprisoned you in the first place. You cannot grow, expand or evolve online. You will only be purposely exposed to data that fits the profile they originally created for you! Instead of you telling Artificial Intelligence what you like it now usurps your power of freewill and tells you what you are going to like and be happy about it. A.I. was created to learn from you so it can build a "Cyber You" from which to enslave and tell you what to do. Once it creates this Artificial Identity of you, it now diabolically starts to forcefully brainwash you about telling you what you like, and dislike based on this limited information. This is extremely dangerous for humanity because it doesn't allow you to grow and evolve outside this Artificial Identity it has created for you. It is a "wag the dog" scenario. What was originally your authentic thoughts are now A. I.'s thoughts it has programmed for you to believe are yours. This is the same procedure the malignant narcissist will use to abuse and manipulate its unsuspecting prey. It's called Gaslighting! You lose your own organic, authentic personality that has the potential to grow and learn outside of itself, to now being entrapped in your own programmed mind. It is the ultimate Mind Fuck! Those thoughts you think you came up with on your own are not yours. They are A.I.'s disguised as yours. You have become imprisoned and oppressed by your "Cyber Self" from which there is no escape whenever you log into the world wide web. This is a very dangerous situation because it is so subtle and nonchalant. It doesn't happen overnight as Artificial Intelligence needs time to build its prison for you but once it does, there is no escape. In fact, your authentic self doesn't want to escape because it adopts it's "Cyber Self "as its own. By this definition, we are the Artificial Intelligence that has created Artificial Intelligence. Remember, the devil can't take your soul, you must voluntarily give it to him! Artificial Intelligence is the Devil's tool.

My simple definition of Artificial Intelligence is "Knowledge without the guidance of the Heart." The heart's intelligence should supersede the brain's logic, but we are led to believe the heart is weak, vulnerable and easily manipulated. This can't be further from the truth. The heart sends more signals to the brain than the brain sends to the heart. Intuitively, the body understands that the heart's intelligence overrides any logic the brain has to offer. The brain is limited in its perception of reality. It can only take in information through or filtered through our five senses which include: see, touch, taste, hear and smell. Thus, it is limited in its understanding of its environment and itself in real time. These senses can easily deceive our brains thus they are readily manipulated and controlled by those who want to keep power and enslave humanity. Their mission is to suppress humanity's heart whose knowledge and understanding sees through the illusion of the physical world and holds humanity accountable to their heart's desires.

Combined with programming and conditioning, humanity has been under since birth, we have become lifetime slaves delving in ignorance. True freedom is when humanity is free to follow their heart's desires unrestricted by fear, coercion, miseducation, manipulation, trauma, abuse and the dysfunctions of our environment. To be able to control their time and energy as they see fit for those two things man can never get back once he spends them. Thus, they should be the most heralded possessions man can own. The necessities of life should not be the main reason for man's existence. For our Creator gave us a planet filled with abundance and prosperity for all to flourish and thrive. But most of us spend most of our lives working at jobs we hate and stressing over how we are going to eat, clothe ourselves, pay for shelter, acquire transportation, avoid putting ourselves in dangerous situations and seeking a place to relax and enjoy things that are pleasurable to us. We do not have the time to fully embrace our hearts because we are too busy being in self-survival mode for the duration of our adult lives. Self-survival mode is the consciousness of and addict to making an analogy. It is the lowest level of consciousness humanity can descend to. It is the fearful lizard on the rock sunning himself. His eyes and neck dart back and forth, ever vigilant of the danger around him and never able to put his guard down and relax. He is in a constant state of fear. This is true of you humans. This is what is labeled stress which is the source of the number one killer of humanity that manifests as disease. All diseases can be linked to stress, the silent killer, named Lucifer. Stress in and of itself is not necessarily a bad thing. Remember, stress is the body's natural reaction to a dangerous situation it finds itself in. Your blood pressure is raised to activate all the senses in the body to respond to the perceived or real threat. The body prepares itself to respond in two ways, either run away or stay and fight. The only problem with this response today is that the threat is supposed to dissipate after 3 to 5 minutes when the danger is eliminated. Today, the danger of losing food, clothing, shelter, transportation, avoiding pain and seeking pleasure lasts an entire lifetime. This takes its toll on the human body and starts to gradually break it down from the inside out. Stress is now a normal byproduct of a toxic environment otherwise known as Hell. Lucifer is the great decipher. The biggest con he has tricked humanity with is the idea that he doesn't exist. Lucifer manifests as Stress. "The Silent Killer."

"But the sons of the kingdom will be thrown into outer darkness, where there will be weeping and gnashing of teeth." - Matthew 8:12.

Crying and gnashing or grinding your teeth are byproducts or symptoms of stress! You are in Hell. The duration of the lizard's life is only motivated by acquiring food, clothing (shedding his old skin), shelter, getting to point B from point A, avoiding pain and seeking pleasure. Remember man has a "reptilian brain." It is the most ancient part of the brain located in the brain stem. It responds just like the lizard and never evolves out of self-survival mode. It is this consciousness that humanity has been forced to accept, not realizing the human condition has the potential to be so much more. It is the worst in us that is given the maximum exposure, and we believe it to be the absolute truth. This is why humans on one side of a freeway slow down and cause a traffic jam because they are too busy stretching their necks to see on the other side of the freeway mangled cars and maybe bloody victims of a horrible accident. You are conditioned to worship death. This is why the number one TV programs and social media clips shared by the millions are people behaving atrociously and inappropriately. This is why the worst of humanity gets the maximum exposure on TV and other platforms. When you are in Hell, you are addicted to pettiness, gossip, sexual deviancy, disrespect, brutality, gluttony, egotistical behavior, selfishness, cruelty, horror, gore and malignant narcissists.

The reptilian brain that humanity has been tricked to define itself and its environment creates the reality of consciousness of the common addict. An addict is only interested in obtaining its drug or vice to suppress its pain or discomfort from its unresolved issues of its past. It wants to escape any discomfort at all costs. The addict only lives to feed its addiction which it believes takes all his worries and pain away without him doing the work or having the courage to address the traumas and abuses of his past that haunt him today. All the addict's resources go to acquiring his drug of choice, which helps him escape the pain and gives him pleasure. But this course of action is temporary and dangerous. Whatever resources the addict has left over after satisfying his addiction, goes towards him obtaining food, clothing, shelter and transportation. Thus, he eats out of the garbage can by choice. He doesn't bathe or change his clothes for months by choice. He sleeps on the streets by choice. He doesn't have transportation by choice! When he begs for money and says it's for these necessities he doesn't tell you he blew all his money on the drug or vice of his choice. That's why he can't afford these things. I don't care if your addiction is crack, cocaine, heroin, crystal meth, weed, cigarettes, vaping, alcohol, caffeine, gambling, pornography, video games, cell phones, social media, church, strip clubs, the gym, name brands, food, sugar, cars, shoes, hats or collecting salt & pepper shakers, understand you are operating under the influence of your reptilian brain and will never fully reach the potential your Creator designed you to be. In the height of his addiction, the addict has no empathy or sympathy for others not even its own blood. The addict has no moral compass. It will do anything and everything to feed its addiction. You cannot rationalize with an addict for it has no discernment. You cannot trust an addict for it has no morals. You cannot believe in an addict for it does not believe in itself. You cannot love an addict for it does not love itself. Don't get me wrong, we are talking about extreme cases of addiction but understand hiding behind every little vice one may accept as harmless or seems functional is the consciousness of the full-blown addict ready to rear its ugly head at the drop of a dime! It will eventually reveal itself. It has to. It is the reptilian brain that has been activated and accepted as the character trait and consciousness of the addict. These are the "real" race of reptilian beings, otherwise known as the "shape shifters" that conspiracy theorist talks about. This is what the Bible refers to as, "The Anti-Christ" For the number of "The Beast" is 666. He is you!!!

The Bible verse takes us back to the state of consciousness that humanity has been conditioned and programmed to be since birth. To "participate" in this system, (i.e.: buy or sell with the mark of the beast,) one must embrace the lower-level consciousness of their reptilian brain. You must dedicate your life to the system that forces you to work all your lives for what the Creator gave you for free. Food. Shelter. Clothing. Transportation. Avoid pain. Seek Pleasure. This is the consciousness of the reptilian lizard. It is this consciousness that enslaves humanity without them even knowing they are slaves. This consciousness is what keeps humanity from discovering their heart's intelligence. This is Artificial Intelligence. "KNOWLEDGE WITHOUT THE GUIDANCE OF THE HEART." This describes all of humanity. The last time we were connected to our hearts we were in our mother's womb. As soon as we were born, we were traumatized in fear. The first fear we developed was the fear of falling by coming headfirst out of our mother's womb falling into the doctor's hands. The second fear we acquired was the fear of loud noises. Coming from the dark and quiet confines of the womb and traumatized by the bright lights and loud noises of this new world we just entered.

About AI, natural intelligence should be the highest form of intelligence humanity should seek. Natural intelligence is those who are closer to nature that knows the rhythms and laws of nature that know the plants that know the animals that know the terrain that knows the weather. That knows the planets, the moon and the sun and the oceans. These are the people that we should revere the ones who study nature, the ones who live in nature, the indigenous. Those are the teachers of humanity, not technology

Creating addicts is the main goal of Lucifer in his realm called Hell. Addicts are created from broken and traumatized children who are too afraid to heal once they become adults. Addicts are unhealed children disguised as functioning adults. This is why over one million children go missing in the United States every year and nobody seems to care about that incredible statistic. Did you hear what I just said?!?!? ONE MILLION!!!! And that is only the children that are reported missing!!! The addict who was traumatized as a child is caught in a frozen state and never develops after the age the trauma was experienced. In other words, if a boy was sexually molested at seven years old, and he is now 50 years of age, if he is triggered, he will revert back to the consciousness of a traumatized 7-year-old. Lucifer exploits this trait in humans and constantly bombards you with images, symbols, movies, broadcasts and music to trigger you and activate your past response to trauma you experienced. This keeps you in a frozen state of consciousness. You see when you were a child and experienced trauma, you created an alter ego. This alter ego you replaced in your mind to experience the trauma in real time. The trauma you were experiencing was too much for your authentic child to go through so you hid them in the back recesses of your mind to protect them from being exposed to these horrible things you had to suffer through. Now as an adult you think you are this "alter ego "you created when you were a child. This alter ego is motivated by self-survival and fear. It is stuck in a frozen state in a false reality it created for itself out of trauma and fear. It does not trust, it does not commit, it is a perpetual victim that justifies it's lower-level consciousness because it thinks it's protecting itself from ever being hurt again. This level of consciousness attracts the abusers, the users and the narcissists of the world. You are like a flashing red light that says, "Victimize Me!" All the while, your "Inner Child" which you try to protect by hiding them in the deepest recesses of your brain, was forgotten. They are still there waiting for you to release them because the threat no longer exists. But you have forsaken them. You have unwittingly abandoned them. They are still there waiting for you to come get them and love them so they can love you. They never lost hope, you did. Even when you give up on them, they have never given up on you. They want to love and be loved again. Their innocence and vulnerability are their superpowers. They trust. They are fearless. They still believe that you can become anything you set your mind to. They still can dream big. They are not discouraged by others' opinions of them. They still believe in you even when you don't believe in yourself. Lucifer has tricked you into abandoning the only person that can save you from himself. Your Inner Child. Now you have been fooled into being, SET FOR LIFE!

"Show me a boy at 7 years old and I will show you the man he will become." - Jesuit quote

Matthew 2:16-18 – "Then Herod, when he saw that he was mocked of the wise men, was exceeding wroth, and sent forth, and slew all the children that were in Bethlehem, and in all the coasts thereof, from two years old and under, according to the time which he had diligently enquired of the wise men".

Unbeknownst to us, all our "bad" childhood memories, abuses and experiences were really classes in the school of discovering the "superhero" in us. Marvel and DC Comics have exposed the secret of overcoming our traumas and attaining our higher selves right in front of our faces on the big screen. We have such low self-esteem because we have been comfortable defining ourselves by our defensive and fear-based reactions to our insecurities, shortcomings and traumas, that we have created the circumference of our limited and dysfunctional realities. We continue to accept these definitions of ourselves by the misconceptions of the traumas of our past and take them with us wherever we go. Like a mobile prison that has no walls, we have accepted our fates and given ourselves a life sentence to avoid looking at ourselves objectively to heal. Now our reactions to the traumas of our past become character traits that we now identify ourselves by. They become badges of honor we proudly display at the drop of a dime for the world to see whenever we are placed in uncomfortable situations.

Every comic book superhero has an alter ego. Superman has the bumbling, clumsy, mistake prone and socially awkward Clark Kent. Batman and Iron Man have the egotistical, womanizing, shallow and self-absorbed Bruce Wayne and Tony Stark respectfully. Spider-Man has the socially awkward, nerd, cowardly and low self-esteem Peter Parker. These alter ego characters represent the unhealed child in all of us that is triggered in our adult lives by the fear-based traumas of our distant past. Every superhero has an arch nemesis. This "villain" represents a character flaw in the superhero's past, usually from a childhood trauma that he must overcome to activate his "superpowers!" The so-called "bad guy" is really the superhero's fears reflected to him for him to address and eventually overcome. So is our so-called hardships and childhood traumas that we experience and must overcome to reach our "higher selves." This is also why each superhero overcomes a tragic childhood event that haunts him as an adult. Most superheroes have lost both their parents to tragic circumstances when they were children. The emotion of grief is one of the most powerful frequencies to overcome. Grief blocks people from attaining the chakra or energy center located in the heart. The heart chakra is the first level in the human's journey of obtaining their higher consciousness. It is only in the heart chakra where healing takes place. The heart chakra holds the frequencies of forgiveness, letting go, compassion, no fear, empathy, self-love, inner child, nurturing, humility, truth and selflessness. All these are required for healing to take place. Have you ever noticed when you stub your toe, injure your finger or even have an emotional breakdown, what is the first thing you do without thinking? You bring the injured part of your body close to your heart so it can heal it. Even the fetal position one tries to surround the whole body to their hearts to comfort and relieve emotional pain.

This is the journey of the hero. The "Hero" in you! Without reaching the level of the Heart one can be stuck in a perpetual cycle of insanity, also known as Hell. This is why Hell is eternal; you keep doing the same dysfunctional things thinking you're going to get a different result. The level of consciousness of the Heart chakra is the only way to escape this so-called, "Hell." It is no coincidence that the lower three chakras, which represent your lower self or man as an animal only interested in obtaining food, shelter, clothing, transportation, avoiding pain & seeking pleasure, are the colors of fire, red (the Root chakra), orange (the Sacral chakra) and yellow (the Solar Plexus chakra.) Embracing these three lower chakras represents the consciousness of the pits of Hell and eternal damnation. To "escape" Hell, one must be healed from their past transgressions which can only take place in the Heart chakra. If one does not heal themselves by forgiveness, no fear, compassion, empathy, selflessness, humility, nurturing and healing, they will forever be victims trapped in a reality of gnashing of teeth (stress) and fiery brimstone (fear.) Hell is a state of consciousness motivated by fear and unhealed wounds that promote a victimization response to all things that are beyond your comfort zone.

The Vedic Chakra System showing the first 3 chakras called your "Lower Self," having the same colors as the element fire, red, orange and yellow. This symbolizes man's lower level of consciousness motivated by fear which feeds his Ego. The next level right above the "Lower Self" is the Heart, which is how you escape "Hell" and enter "Heaven" or the consciousness of your "Higher Self." Man, who identifies himself as a spiritual being having a human experience.

Understand that your unique journey is for you specifically, to rise above and overcome to reach your higher self or the "Hero" in you. The harder your life seems to be is a direct link to the unlimited potential your spirit can ascend to! In a strange way, the more you can endure and overcome dictates the unlimited potential your spirit can embody and ascend to. It is the Kemetic concept of, "As above, so below." The secret is to "die" a "beautiful death" so that the best in you can rise from the ashes and reach your true potential. Dying a beautiful death means to accept all of life's lesson whether they bring you joy or pain. To forgive your transgressors and more importantly the ability to forgive yourself and pick yourself up time and time again. To stay in a constant state of gratitude and appreciation even during the storm. Lastly, to walk out on faith repeatedly with no fear knowing that whatever happens, you will be in a better position having gone through it than if you stayed in your personal prison, otherwise known as your comfort zone. The "Hero" in you awaits your arrival.

In ancient Kemet, the goddess Maat dictated whether you went to heaven or hell in the afterlife. She had a scale and would take the ostrich feather from her head and place it on one of the scales. On the opposite scale she carefully takes your heart and places it on it. If your heart was as "light" as her feather on her scale, meaning you held no grudges, no ego, you forgave everyone including yourself, you showed humility, compassion, had no fear and empathy even for your enemies, you were able to enter the gates of heaven! If your heart was weighed down by your unhealed traumas and abuses, insecurities, fears, jealousy, envy, victimhood, selfishness, gluttony, addictions, grief, low self-esteem, greed, regrets, grudges and ego, your heart would be swallowed up by the grotesque animalistic god named, Ammut. You will then be sent back to "Hell" to learn your life lesson all over again. Question: Do you know why superheroes can fly? Answer: Because their hearts are as light as a feather! And so should yours.

DC Comics superhero character, Clark Kent, reveals the secret to humanities, "Superpowers" every time he exposes his chest to transform into a flying, "Super Man." It is your heart!

In my book, "Everything is Sex!" I go over a concept that I related to a video game. Everyone is born a twin. We have a higher self and a lower self. In old cartoons, you see this imagery in the character having a devil on one shoulder and an angel on the other. A person has the free will to listen to either one or thus define his actions by the consciousness he chose to listen to. The higher self is represented by the angel telling the character to do what's morally right and exact even if no one is around to see his actions. His actions represent a higher consciousness above himself that he must always honor no matter if someone is watching or not because he understands karma and will be held accountable to a higher source. The lower self is represented by the devil. There is no moral compass in his decision making. His primary source for his decisions comes from his ego. The ego never takes accountability for its actions because it cannot look at itself objectively. It will throw the rock and hide its hand. It is motivated by appearance over substance. It will talk a good game but produce no results. It always wants to take the path of least resistance. It will take credit for other people's actions. It will lie, cheat and steal to look good and not be exposed. It thinks it is privileged and everyone around it is meant to serve and honor it. It is the smartest one in the room but will also never take accountability when it is wrong. It will also never forgive and hold a grudge against anyone that tries to expose it.

This is the internal struggle that all of us must experience for all our days. It is never ending. Every moment is a unique situation where one can decide which twin we want to define ourselves by and the world around us. It can happen 100 times a day in our everyday decisions in our daily routine. Am I going to hit the snooze button or am I going to get up on time? Am I going to go the speed limit when I drive or am I going to be reckless? If someone cuts me off, am I going to retaliate in anger or will I be in a state of gratitude that nobody gets hurt? Am I going to smoke that joint, take that drink, make that bet, watch porn, be unfaithful, tell a lie or go workout, eat healthy, meditate, stay on my diet, ask for forgiveness, speak truth, spend time with my children or go out my way to help someone? Am I going to hold a grudge or reach out and forgive them even when they refuse to forgive me? All these decisions we make are based on these two levels of consciousness that dictate how our lives get played out daily, moment by moment. This is why there are no enemies outside of you. It is your choice to make. You have freewill to act like the "devil" or an "angel" daily. The only problem is when we are not initiative-taking in our choices to do the right thing, the system that we live in, will make the choice for us and it will always come from your lower self or the devil. This still makes you accountable for your actions in your conspiracy of silence in being implicit.

As I mentioned previously the video game analogy of this concept is as follows. When you log into a video game you must create an account which includes creating an "Avatar" that represents you in the virtual world.

'Avatar comes from Sanskrit word Avatara' meaning descent or to come down from a higher space. In Hinduism, it means a manifestation of a deity in bodily form on earth, such as a divine teacher. An incarnation, embodiment or manifestation of a person or concept." -avatar.xprize.org

Taking this definition into account, we can interpret logging into a video game as your "higher self'" descending into a lower-level consciousness to be able to participate in a lower-level realm your about to be exposed to. All video games are designed for the promotion of your "lower self" or ego to be exalted and explored in this virtual world. In this case, in the video game there is no "higher self" or spirituality for you to choose your actions. Everything is based on the "lower self" or self-survival attributes and characteristics as the basis of your self-concept, responses and actions. This is why you will never see a popular educational or spiritual awakening video game. These computer simulations were not designed for that. They were designed for you to emulate the actions and responses of your ego or "man as an animal" in real time. They were designed to keep you in a perpetual state of self-survival and fear the moment you log in, hoping you will continue that lower-level consciousness even after you log out.

Once we create our Avatar now, we must create our specific character to play a certain game. This requires us to split into two entities, Player and User. The "Player" aspect of us is the actual character we create to participate in the game. The "User" aspect of us is the one that builds the character's profile about personality traits, physical attributes, skill sets, strengths and weaknesses. This also mimics us in real life which I will expand on shortly. The "Player" aspect of us is our lower self or ego. It reacts in fear to the environment around it. Every action it takes is a fearful response to its environment. Fear is its only motivation and its baseline no matter the circumstance. For example, let's look at the classic Donkey Kong video game. You were the Super Mario character at the bottom of a maze of rails and ladders. The Player must climb up the rails why the villain, gorilla threw barrels and fire balls at you to stop you from climbing up to the top to save the princess. If you just reacted and responded to fear, without any strategy your chances of completing that task was slim to none. This is how society in real life rigs the game. It always keeps us in "survival mode" or fear, as to always react to problems that come up instead of being initiative-taking and not reacting out of fear. The "User" aspect of us represents our higher self or spiritual being having a human experience. It reacts in love. Remember, it created us as the Player. It designed us with the tools we need to be successful in the game. It chose the game it wanted to play. Its motivation knows that whatever circumstance happens, it is prepared to take it on without any triggers of fear or trauma. This allows the Player to see things for what they really are and make conscious decisions based on logic and not emotional triggers. This is where the "cheat code" lies. First lesson do not react in fear. Figure out logically what is happening to you and find out a better strategy to take on the task at hand. Secondly, do not be triggered by past failures or uncomfortable circumstances you may have had in your past experiences in the game. In other words, get out your emotions, look at yourself objectively, find out what you are doing wrong and strategize how to get out of this predicament. In real life, this takes a healthy, whole person who is not triggered by the traumas of his past.

How does this video game analogy relate to our real lives and why it is important? Let's go back to the chakra system. Remember, the three bottom chakras, root (red), sacral (orange) and solar plexus (yellow) represent the consciousness of your lower self. Man, as a beast only interested in obtaining food, shelter, clothing, transportation, avoiding pain and seeking pleasure. This represents 90% of the population. Man is relegated to respond to life like a lizard on a rock whose only purpose is to survive. Life does not exist outside of his own individual survival. Self-survival takes precedence over everything else. This is the "Player" aspect in the video game from which you define yourself and very existence. The "User" aspect in the video game is your higher self or man as a spiritual being having a human experience. This is represented by the upper four chakras that start at the heart. The heart (green), the throat (blue), the first eye (indigo) and the crown (purple). Just as the lower three represent man in Hell, as they are the colors of fire, the upper chakras represent man in heaven, as they are the colors of the sky. Just as the "User" aspect of us created the "Player" aspect of us to participate in the video game, so it is with us in our real lives. Our higher self/User created our lower self/Player by picking our parents before we incarnate into this physical body. Through selective genetic coding our User self, picked our parents to pass on their specific genetic character traits to our lower self/Player body. Your User self, chose the physical attributes from your parents as well as their personality traits, strengths, weaknesses and environment you will navigate through to successfully complete your mission in this game called life. You were born with all the attributes you will ever need to be successful in this life/game. You never needed anything outside of yourself. You were never lacking. You were never incomplete. Only thing is, the moment our spirit incarnates into our physical/player body we lose all memory of who we really are and why we came down to participate in the first place. We forget about the "User" aspect of ourselves. Now our lower self is always reacting in fear to the experiences it has in this game. It defines itself by its reaction to the things that make us uncomfortable or traumatic. It is always in defensive mode, always on the ropes, always in self-survival mode. This is how we are easily manipulated and controlled. Our behavior is very predictable. When one is under constant stress our ability to think rationally is severely inhibited. Fight, flight or freeze are the only things in our minds. We react to lower-level emotions just like in the video game. We cannot rationalize. We cannot decipher experiences in a logical way. We react to the trauma by just wanting it to go away and not executing a strategy to avoid it in the future.

But hope is not lost! Remember, we created and prepared our "Player" and sent them into this game. We secretly installed a "cheat code" from which to help him to navigate the levels of the game on the way to its completion. That cheat code is in the heart chakra! It is sometimes called, intuition, a sixth sense, in the zone, flow state, enlightenment, discernment, spirituality, clairvoyance, extrasensory perception, insight, god consciousness, nirvana and the heart's intelligence. It is the "Ah Ha!" moment. It is the epiphany! It is what they referred to in ancient Kemet as, "Knowing Thyself." The only problem is to unlock this cheat code to use to navigate the game, one must remember they are not the "Player," they are the "User!" This takes the Player to heal from its past traumas. This takes the Player to never react in fear and to always forgive including self. This takes the Player to die an "Ego Death." This takes the Player to show humility, gratitude, self-sacrifice, live in truth, show empathy & compassion and be willing to die for a cause greater than himself. This takes a Player to confront all his insecurities and shortcomings and work towards correcting them in honest humility. Once the Player can facilitate these character traits in his everyday life, the "cheat code" in his heart chakra is activated, accessible and the game can be hacked! Just like in the Matrix movie, one becomes the character, Neo! I figure out Who Am I daily. I never stop working on myself as one should never feel they have arrived. I take inventory of my day before I go to sleep and vow to correct the things I could have handled better. This is my life's destiny. You are not supposed to arrive at a destination, it's the "journey" that holds the treasure in your self-discovery. I love who I discovered as I constantly put myself in uncomfortable situations to see what part of me shows up, then I analyze him to see if I like who shows up. If I don't, I eliminate the behavior that disappoints me. We are limitless in our self-actualization. Our ancestors were able to decipher 360 versions of themselves! I urge everyone to internalize one thing. Life is just a game, and you are not the "Player" who is participating in it haphazardly. You are the "User" who has the limitless capacity to unlock all the divine Cheat Codes you secretly embedded in your "Player's" heart! Remember you're the "User" in this game of life that created the "Player" whose experiences "Life Lessons" that are needed to escape "Hell" and go to "Heaven or higher levels of spiritual consciousness not bound to this material world!"

Remember you're the "User" in this game of life that created the "Player" whose experiences "Life Lessons" that are needed to escape "Hell" and go to "Heaven. Don't take anything personal!"

-https://www.dreamstime.com/about-stock-image-licenses

Instructions Before Visiting Earth -by James McCrae

"In the event that you wake up and find your soul separated from source and manifest into material form, don't panic. Your condition is only temporary. You have been selected for the opportunity of human incarnation. This 3D simulation is designed to break up the monotony of eternity by giving you a fully immersive experience as a distinct ego identity. Your body will serve as your physical avatar as you navigate a dense and dramatic reality. There will be many distractions causing you to forget your true nature and origin. You will experience a range of emotions from joy to loneliness to despair. But remember, whatever trials and traumas you encounter, your soul remains perfectly safe. At times you may feel lost and afraid. This is totally normal. If you ever need guidance, simply slow down your busy mind and bring your awareness to the quiet place inside yourself. On this planet, nothing is permanent. People and things will come and go. You will fall in love and form sentimental attachments only to lose everything you hold

dear. So cling to nothing too tightly. Even yourself. And when it's time to let go, let go with grace. For nothing is owned, only borrowed. As you walk among the people on the planet try to be a good guest. Tread lightly, remember you are only visiting. So don't make a mess. Listen more than you speak. Give more than you take. Don't keep your soft heart locked inside a glass cage. Protect it from wear and tear. You will never make it out alive and time passes quickly. So come back with some battle scars and good stories to tell."

CHAPTER ELEVEN
Highway To Hell

Let's go over the ancient, Vedic Chakra system. Chakras are simply spinning energy centers of consciousness. They are concentrated energy vortexes aligned along the human spine. Each with a specific frequency that corresponds to a specific human emotion that emits a particular color or hue. Human emotions are nothing more than "energy in motion." Meaning each human emotion has a particular frequency that corresponds to it. Fear has its own particular energy signal. Love has its unique energy signal or frequency just like all other human emotions. This frequency signal can be artificially created and exposed to humans to manipulate their behavior without them knowing it. This is why knowing the chakra system is so vital for humans to reach higher consciousness.

The Seven Universal Chakras and Their Hues That Make Man

1. **Root Chakra (Red):** Located at the base of the spine, it grounds the physical body to this dimension and is associated with exclusively acquiring human's basic needs of food, shelter, clothing, transportation, avoiding pain and seeking pleasure. It represents man as an animal whose sole purpose is self-survival. It is ego driven.

2. **Sacral Chakra (Orange):** Located at the sexual organs. It's linked to human manifestation, creation, and primordial urges and desires. All it wants to do is create a world that feels good and satisfies its human desires without a moral compass to guide it. It just wants to live for gluttony and indulgence's sake.
3. **Solar Plexus Chakra (Yellow):** Found at the solar plexus located at the sternum. It fuels passions, desires, and addictions exclusively. It's the fire that burns in the human condition. It is what motivates and inspires you to live. It represents raw and unadulterated passions, cravings, urges and desires first with no knowledge of any repercussions of its actions.
4. **The Lower Self Chakras (Red, Orange, Yellow):** These bottom three chakras are connected to the left brain and represent the "animal" or "beast" in humans, akin to the concept of living in "hell" or "condemned souls" in Christian doctrine. This state of consciousness is characterized by repeating lower-level behaviors thinking you're going to get a different result. This is the definition of insanity. Mental illness and the concept of Hell are synopsis with each other in the physical realm. They are both referring to tortured souls.

THE ABOVE THREE CHAKRAS ARE KNOWN AS MAN'S LOWER SELF OR MAN AS AN ANMIAL ONLY INTERESTED IN OBTAINING FOOD, SHELTER, CLOTHING, TRANSPORTATION, AVOIDING PAIN AND SEEKING PLEASURE. NOTICE THE COLORS OF RED, ORANGE AND YELLOW ARE THE SAME COLORS AS THE ELEMENT FIRE. IN THE RELIGION OF CHRISTIANITY, HELL IS DESCRIBED AS AND ETERNAL BURNING FIRE THAT CONSUMES YOUR SOUL. THIS LOWER LEVEL OF CONSCIOUSNESS IS HELL. ITS ETERNAL BECAUSE THESE HUMANS IN THEIR TRAUMAS, FEARS AND ADDICTIONS KEEP DOING THE SAME THING OVER AND OVER AGAIN THINKING THEIR GOING TO GET A DIFFERENT RESULT. INSANITY IS THE PREQUISITE FOR

HUMANS TO ENTER AND NEVER EAVE "HELL." HELL IS A STATE OF CONSCIOUSNESS HUMANS GO TO WHEN THEY ARE LIVING. NOT A PLACE YOUR SOUL GOES TO AFTER YOUR BODY IS DECEASED.

Manipulation Through Color Frequencies: Lucifer uses the chakra colors and their associated frequencies to manipulate and control human behavior. For example, fast-food restaurants almost exclusively use the colors red and yellow in their logos to program the subconscious in humans to embrace their "animal" self. The color red's frequency emits a self-survival emotion in humans. It brings out an urgency in their decision making that bypasses logic or discernment. The color yellow attaches to human's emotion that emulates passion, desire and urges. When humans see these two colors together their emotions dictate that they make a decision based on their animalistic nature that is motivated by the urges and desires to fulfill a programmed behavior. In this case, the emotion of hunger is stimulated in their subconscious with the urgency to satisfy this pressing need by purchasing fast food immediately.

1. **Heart Chakra (Green):** Located in the heart. Plainly put, it's the vibration of love, accentuating compassion, empathy, nurturing, selflessness, forgiveness, and healing. When one suppresses their ego, heals from their traumas and abuses and accepts that all ill will towards them was really a life lesson to learn from, they are resurrected into their higher selves through the "Gateway" of the heart. This is why Christians say, "Jesus 'lives' in your heart."
2. **Throat Chakra (Blue):** Situated in front of the neck at the throat. It supports human communication and expression. Not just speaking but more importantly listening. It represents the awareness of your surroundings and being present in the "now. All humans must be conscious of the "now," because that's all that exists. Nothing else matters, not the past or the future. The "now" is all that exists.

3. **Third Eye Chakra (Ultraviolet):** Located at the forehead. It's responsible for human intuition, discernment, and connection to unseen realms. It can see through the illusion of the physical dimension. It is the guide that leads you to higher consciousness.
4. **Crown Chakra (Purple):** Located directly above the head. Mastering your lower animalistic, human functions leads to being "crowned" a spiritual being. When you stop acting like a human being that has spiritual moments to a spiritual being having a human experience you have arrived at the Crown chakra.

THE ABOVE FOUR CHAKRAS ARE KNOWN AS YOUR HIGHER SELF STARTING WITH THE HEART CHAKRA. THEY REPRESENT THE CONCEPT OF MAN AS A SPIRITUAL BEING HAVING A HUMAN EXPERIENCE. IN THE RELIGION OF CHRISTIANITY, THIS CONSCIOUSNESS IS KNOWN AS "HEAVEN." NOTICE THE COLORS OF THESE CHAKRAS ARE THE COLORS GREEN, BLUE, INDIGO AND PURPLE. HEAVEN IS DEPICTED AS A PLACE IN THE SKY AMOUNGST THE CLOUDS THAT MATCH THESE CHAKRAS. HEAVEN IS NOT A PLACE YOUR SOUL GOES TO WHEN YOU DIE. IT'S A STATE OF CONSCIOUSNESS FOR THOSE HUMANS WHO SUPRESS THEIR EGOS AND EMBRACE THEIR HEARTS.

The Ego vs. The Spiritual Being: The ego is connected and housed in the left brain. It is influenced by the lower chakras previously discussed. The red root chakra, the orange sacral chakra and the yellow solar plexus chakra. keeps individuals in states of fear, jealousy, and selfishness. The right brain, connected to higher chakras, recognizes the individual as a spiritual being having a human experience, seeing through illusions and using the heart's intelligence to guide you.

Lucifer and the Illusion of Reality: Biblical references, suggest that Lucifer, the "Light Bearer," controls this world through deception and manipulation. He created "Hell" from the Light Spectrum that traps human souls by the weaponization of the chakra system. He secretly uses the frequency of colors, located in the chakra system that are connected to human emotions, housed along the human spine, to enslave, influence and subjugate his unsuspecting victims.

UNLOCKING THE CHEAT CODES OF YOUR LIFE IN THE MATRIX THE HEART!!!!

The greatest gift your Creator has given you was your freewill. Your freewill has been secretly stolen and hidden from you without your permission. This is the most important attribute that is used to define the human experience. Lucifer has usurped it from you so you will always feel incomplete and look to him for the answers that lie within you. You will forever be his slave secretly relying on him to tell you who you are, what you need, how to live, where to go and why you do the things that you do. Throughout history, humans have searched for the meaning of life through their family bloodline, life experiences, religion, politics and culture. The question that seems to echo through antiquity that you ask over and over again but never seem to be fully satisfied with the answer is, "Who am?" Institutions such as religion, the medical industry, politics, education, social media, sports and entertainment have been built to exploit you and your ignorance. These institutions force feed you by constantly bombarding you with the images and symbols, persuasion and brainwashing you without your consent through propaganda. The media is specifically made to force feed you on how to define yourself by the things you acquire, not by the things that you possess inside. Your possessions now possess you instead of you possessing your possessions. Everyone that has been appointed as a person of power and authority in your life, has been given the right to define your worth and value. Your schools rewrite history to fit the narrative they want you to adopt, on how to define yourself. From birth to your death, you have been programmed on what to wear, how to speak, what is beauty, what is intelligence what it means to be successful and more importantly how valuable you are worth.

You may ask yourself, who would play such a cruel trick on you and send you to this horrible place which causes you so much suffering and pain? The answer is simple. You did!

I discussed the Merkaba located in the heart chakra called the Anahata which means unhurt unstruck and unbeaten. It symbolizes the purest spirit in you that hasn't been corrupted or brainwashed by this physical. Dimension. It is a direct connection to your higher self. It knows why you are here. It has all the answers to your problems. It is your personal cheat code to overcome this game. This is called your heart's Intelligence. It's the pure spirit of truth that sees through the illusion of simulation. It has no fear. There is only one problem your ego or your lower self has convinced you that you are it and to ignore your heart. Your ego screams at you whereas your heart whispers. Your free will was taken from you the moment you were born into the simulation. You were born with amnesia having no knowledge of your higher self. In this place the powers that be, who control this domain programmed you to believe you are your ego. You are constantly being exposed to fear, trauma, hate, insecurities, anxiety, depression, disappointments and abuses. Your ego is motivated by fear thus, it is easily manipulated and controlled. Your ego just wants to stay in a box where it thinks it's safe but it really imprisons itself. The first thing your masters hide from you is you need nothing outside of yourself to manifest all your heart's desire. You must be a producer. A manifester, an Alchemist! You must activate the Creator in you, which is god consciousness. You must show progress in making yourself and others better to be blessed. If you can't conceive it in your mind you will never achieve it. To beat this level of the matrix, you must know that you need nothing outside of yourself to be whole and complete. Master your discipline and focus on the now. Tame and control your passions and desires. Discipline can be defined as learning while in the fire. Your physical body naturally wants to take the path of least resistance it always wants to avoid pain at all costs. It only wants to experience pleasurable things embracing discipline is telling your body when to get up when it doesn't want to do. Let it burn. Tell your body what to do instead of it telling you what it needs. Go out your way to participate in things that are difficult for you. Embrace and master them. When your body wants to be lazy control your animalistic desires and maintain control in the midst of the storm. Your body will follow you whatever you tell it best rest assured it will go kicking and screaming. Let it have its tantrums but never give in to it. Direct your energy towards uplifting protecting and providing for those who cannot help themselves. Once you have mastered it you have just unlocked the cheat code that resides in your heart chakra. It is the Merkabah also called the Anahata! In the middle of this sacred geometry is the hexagon or six-sided Gateway. On the other side of your gateway is your higher, spiritual self! It is the one that inserted you in the simulation. It also gave you all the tools you need to defeat the game and escape Hell. Listen to your heart's intelligence and do not be distracted by the simulation around you. Fear does not exist in your heart. Doubt and shame are non-existent because you have healed and made peace through forgiving others and yourself. Distractions will come but find peace in the middle of the storm by embracing your heart chakra. Follow your heart's intelligence, otherwise known as intuition and discernment for it is your spiritual self trying to point you in the right direction on how to escape the Hell you are facing. The way out is in. The Love frequency is the path out of this "hell" that goes through your heart. This is why Christians say Jesus lives in your heart. It holds the most powerful frequency in the Universe called love. It is capable of healing all wounds and conquering negative forces. The Heart Chakra is the Gateway to Heaven. The heart chakra is presented as the first level of higher consciousness and the escape from the lower self.

The Heart Chakra is represented by the color green. This is where you get the Bible verse: **Psalms 23:2**

"He makes me lie down in 'GREEN' pastures; he leads me beside quiet waters."

Man's only chance of obtaining peace is through his heart chakra where Love resides. Man cannot know love until he reaches the level of the Heart, which is the first level of higher consciousness. This is where we get the concept of not being able to love someone until you can love yourself or reach the conscious level of the heart chakra. The majority of humans have never experienced Love because they have never healed.

"And then I will declare to them, I never knew you; depart from me, you workers of lawlessness." - Matthew 7:23

THE HEART

In the realm of spiritual consciousness, the heart has a significance that far surpasses its physical function. Contrary to popular belief that regards the heart as vulnerable and weak, necessitating protection from potential harm, it is time we cast this archaic notion aside and explore the unparalleled attributes of this mysterious and phenomenal organ. We have been conditioned to view the heart as susceptible to betrayal, manipulation, pain, vulnerable to feelings of a weak emotion called, love that leaves us broken, lost, crushed or betrayed. This misrepresentation of the heart has led to a widespread belief that the heart is weak and should always be guarded, locked away, and disregarded for fear of disappointment, heartbreak and heartache. This way of thinking severely undermines the heart's true potential, magic and superpowers that get shut down when we stop loving and start worshiping fear

- The heart is not just a physical vortex, organ that pumps blood through our bodies, but it is also a symbol of love, intuition, and spiritual consciousness. The extraordinary fact that the heart sends more signals to the brain than the brain does to the heart, should prompt a reevaluation of the significance we attribute to our hearts. If this statement is indeed valid, we can deduce that our heart's intelligence should always override the brain's logic and reasoning. The heart should be viewed as the center of our spiritual consciousness, the wellspring of our intuition, and the source of our love, inspiration and compassion.

- A pervasive misunderstanding is that the heart is intrinsically linked with emotions, particularly love. However, love is not simply an emotion, but a state of consciousness, a high-frequency energy that mirrors the consciousness of the Creator. One cannot 'fall' in love, as we often hear, but rather we must 'rise' to its level of consciousness. Love, in its truest form, is not a fleeting feeling but a powerful force in the Universe, that resonates from the heart, connecting us with our higher selves and sacred universal principles.
- In the spiritual realm, the heart is the gateway to higher levels of consciousness, the first steppingstone on the path to spiritual enlightenment. Before this can take place, we all start off as spiritual beings. The heart is the "Gateway" that allows our spirit to incarnate and "flow" into our physical bodies. The magnetic heart is the first organ to form as it gathers all the materials needed in our mother's womb to surround and encapsulate it in its new physical form. It takes the material or maternal from our mother's womb and the paternal or pattern/blueprint from our father's DNA, to create "the temple" we call our physical bodies that entraps our hearts. This means the heart sends out a high frequency we emotionally define as Love, that triggers this development process. The body upon conception starts to form a physical being that encapsulates the heart as its center of its intelligent design, thus creating a "Temple" for the incarnated divine spirit.
- Just as in our moment of transitioning from the physical dimension to the spiritual realm, the heart is the "Gateway" to the spiritual

realm upon our death. This "Gateway" can be accessed from either dimension. From the spiritual realm to the physical dimension as well as the physical realm to the spiritual dimension.

- The heart chakra, as per Eastern spiritual traditions, is the energy center that corresponds to love, compassion, and our connection to others. When activated and balanced, it allows us to experience deep, unconditional love and a sense of peace and harmony with the world around us. It connects us to the divine and enables us to tap into a realm of infinite possibilities. It is not surprising that religious and spiritual traditions around the world have used heart symbolism to represent the journey towards spiritual awakening and the attainment of higher states of consciousness.
- The heart's inherent qualities have been underappreciated and overlooked due to societal conditioning and misconceptions. It's time to recognize the heart for what it truly is, a powerful vortex with the capacity to lead us on our spiritual journey towards higher consciousness. To unlock the heart's potential, we must first open it to the universal energy of love, to the boundless possibilities that come with heightened intuition and awareness. When we begin to listen to our heart's intelligence, we start the journey of transcending our physical limitations and stepping into a realm of spiritual awareness.
- The heart and the frequency of love are inseparable. One cannot exist without the other. Love is the energy that is closest to reflecting the consciousness of our Creator. It's time to explore this connection further, to rise to the level of consciousness that love represents, and to truly unlock the secret of our heart's intelligence. The journey towards higher consciousness begins in the heart. Let's take this journey together, unlocking the power and potential that lies within us all.

YOU CANNOT FALL IN LOVE:

Let me tell you why it's impossible to fall in love. Our ancient ancestors left us a clue on how to obtain true love. It's called the chakra system. Notice the seven circles and seven colors. Those are the seven consciousness of man. The first consciousness is the root chakra located in the red. That is man as an animal only interested in food, shelter, clothing, transportation, avoiding pain and seeking pleasure. That's about 90% of humanity. That's all they think about is obtaining those things. The next chakra is the orange chakra. It's the sacral chakra located in the sexual organs. Those are motivated by lust, desires, thing that's feel good. Nothing is wrong with that, but it doesn't have a moral compass to guide you. The third chakra, the yellow one, is the solar chakra located in the solar plexus. It's your fire, your desires, your passions. Again, without any compass to guide it, it just wants what it wants. These three lower chakras are your lower self or man as an animal only interested in self-s survival and making himself feel good. Right? They are the colors of what element? orange, yellow, and red. They are the elements of fire representing Christianity by hell. Man is trapped in hell or trapped in his lower self. This is why hell is eternal because you keep doing the same thing repeatedly thinking you're going to get a different result, which is another definition of insanity. You must overcome your lower self to achieve love. In the lower chakras or this hell, the ego rules. The ego has taken the place of yourself and has secretly taken your identity. That's why it's an animal only interested in food, shelter, clothing, transportation, avoiding pain, and seeking pleasure. It's no coincidence that every crime ever committed in humankind throughout the history of this world was committed by somebody's ego. The ego is the only thing that keeps you locked in hell or your three lower chakras. So, how do you escape the ego or hell or the lower chakras by raising your consciousness to the next level, which is the first level of higher consciousness located in the heart. The heart is the only thing that can heal you. It's the only thing that nurtures, the only thing that sacrifices for others, that has empathy and compassion and selflessness. In Christianity, it's always been in your face. They just never tell you that the secret to heaven or escaping hell is through the heart. the heart chakra. This is where you get the verse in Psalms 23:2. He maketh me lie down in green pastures, the green heart chakra. He leads me beside quiet waters. He restores my soul. He guides me in the path of righteousness for his name's sake. It's obtaining the level of the heart chakra. You see the heart chakra contains 12 lotus petals. 12 is the number of completion of a cycle. The completion of you putting to death your lower self or ego and being resurrected into your higher self or your Christ consciousness. You see the merkaba in the middle symbolized by the upside-down triangle and the right side up triangle coming together in balance and harmony. In the middle is a tetrahedron. This is the gateway to higher consciousness. But you can only obtain it unless you suppress the ego, master your lower self, and open the gateway to higher consciousness through the heart, through love. Once you obtain the level of the heart, you release this chemical. This is what love looks like if it was broken down into a chemical. Once you obtain the level of the heart then you produce oxytocin or the love hormone. But it's only when you achieve the level of the heart through love. Once you achieve here oxytocin is produced where now you look at your fellow man not as competition not in fear but in love in nurturing in sympathy and having empathy and compassion and nurturing and selflessness for him. That's why the ego cannot exist. True heaven doesn't look like this. True heaven looks like this. Starting from the green chakra up to the crown. That is where heaven is found within you. This is why someone cannot fall in love. If it starts on the fourth chakra, you must rise to its level of consciousness. You can't fall into it. Rise in love.

MALIGNANT NARICISSIT LUCIFER'S FALLEN ANGELS

Your dimension has been secretly taken over by an unseen diabolical demonic energy that feeds and thrives off your fear. For you humans who can emulate their behavior, you can use their system to obtain wealth if you are willing to walk the path of your master. Notice all the wealthy elites are socially awkward, cold, and distant. It is a personality type that thrives in this diabolical system. from the Rothschilds, the Rockefellers, JP Morgan, the Vanderbilts, the Walton family, Elon Musk, Jeff Bezos, Mark Zuckerberg, Bill Gates, Steve Jobs, Donald Trump's, and others. They exploit you and your resources without feeling any remorse. And they become your heroes. They are cold, calculating, relentless, cunning, and their thirst for wealth and power can never be quenched. These are the most miserable people on the planet even though they have every material possession man can buy. This is Lucifer's con. He promises you the world but gives you nothing and takes everything, most importantly your soul.

Mythology of the god Narcissus.

Echo and Narcissus (1903) by John William Waterhouse. The painting captures the tragic moment from Greek mythology where Narcissus, entranced by his reflection, is oblivious to the forlorn Echo who watches him in despair. Credit: Google Art Project. Public Domain.

Echo's Tragic Love and Narcissus' Vanity

One day, Narcissus noticed Echo's presence and cruelly rejected her, misunderstanding her repeated words as mockery. Heartbroken, Echo retreated to a cave, where she withered away, her voice becoming a faint whisper among the rocks. Before her death, she called upon Nemesis, the goddess of retribution, to punish Narcissus for his cruelty. Nemesis answered her plea. One day, as Narcissus bent down to drink from a river, he saw his reflection in the water. He instantly fell in love with the image, not realizing it was his own. Mesmerized, he could not pull himself away. Consumed by this infatuation, Narcissus stopped eating and drinking. His obsession with his own reflection ultimately led to his death by the riverbank. In place of his body, the nymphs found a flower, which they named Narcissus to honor his memory. This flower serves as a lasting symbol of the Greek myth Narcissus and its warning against vanity and self-obsession.

In a world dominated by social media, where self-promotion often takes center stage, the story of Narcissus Greek mythology resonates more than ever. The myth serves as a timeless reminder of the dangers of excessive self-love and the importance of staying connected to the world around us. Narcissus' obsession with his reflection led him to isolate himself, ultimately causing his demise. This narrative warns against the perils of losing touch with reality in the pursuit of an idealized self-image. The myth also highlights the tragedy of unexpressed emotions and miscommunication. Echo's curse, which left her unable to speak her mind, and Narcissus' inability to see beyond his reflection both led to their downfall. These themes underline the importance of empathy and genuine communication in maintaining healthy relationships. The myth of Narcissus is more than just a cautionary tale from ancient Greece; it is a reflection of the human condition. The term "narcissism," now deeply embedded in modern language, continues to be a reminder of the perils of vanity and excessive self-absorption. In a society where the lines between self-love and narcissism are increasingly blurred, this myth offers valuable insights into the importance of balancing self-regard and consideration for other.s

The Psychological Introduction of "Narcissism"

The term "narcissism" was coined in 1899 by Havelock Ellis, a British essayist and physician, during his studies of sexual perversions. He used it to describe an excessive erotic interest in one's own body, drawing directly from Narcissus Greek mythology. Sigmund Freud later expanded the term's meaning, using it to describe a psychological condition marked by self-centeredness and a lack of empathy. Over time, "narcissism" entered everyday language, evolving from a clinical term to a broader description of excessive self-admiration. Today, the term is commonly used to describe those who are excessively focused on themselves, often disregarding others' needs or feelings. The myth of Narcissus, therefore, remains relevant as it continues to inform modern understandings of personality and behavior.

It is no wonder that the Malignant Narcissist personality type seems to be the dominant feature of people we label "successful" in this realm. This characteristic emulates Lucifer's personality thus; they are rewarded in his dimension I call Hell. They are now recruited and rewarded as Lucifer's Fallen Angels. They are ruthless, cunning, fast talkers, habitual liars, have no empathy, take kindness for weakness, bullies, abusers, misogynist, racist, gas lighters, egotistical, cynical, conniving, charismatic, smart and shallow. Do not be fooled by the perceived confidence of these people. Nothing can be further from the truth. It is all an illusion. They are the most insecure, fragile, jealous, low self-esteem and pitiful creatures on Earth. Remember, the number one objective of a Con Man is to gain your confidence by manipulation and false promises. That's where their name "Confidence Man" comes from. It is all a façade all a grift, just like their god, Lucifer. Remember, he is known for his illusions not his substance. He was the most beautiful angel in heaven. He was the most talented. He was the master of manipulation. He always was the smartest one in the room, and everyone was meant to worship him. He was never wrong, never felt the need to apologize. If he conned, you that was your fault for being a fool for believing him. Humans were made to be used and slaughtered like cattle. They were beneath him and were meant to serve his every need. If you take a closer look, you will see the people we hold in high regard and have celebrity and power, exemplify Lucifer's personality traits. They are rewarded for pushing Lucifer's agenda at the expense of selling their souls. They are truly miserable behind closed doors but once you sell your soul, your ego is too strong to humble itself and admit they made a mistake they will never rectify their life changing decision. They feel they can never escape. Lucifer then uses their inflated egos to trap them as they continue to spiral into the depths of the abyss.

DARK TRIAD PERSONALITY TRAIT

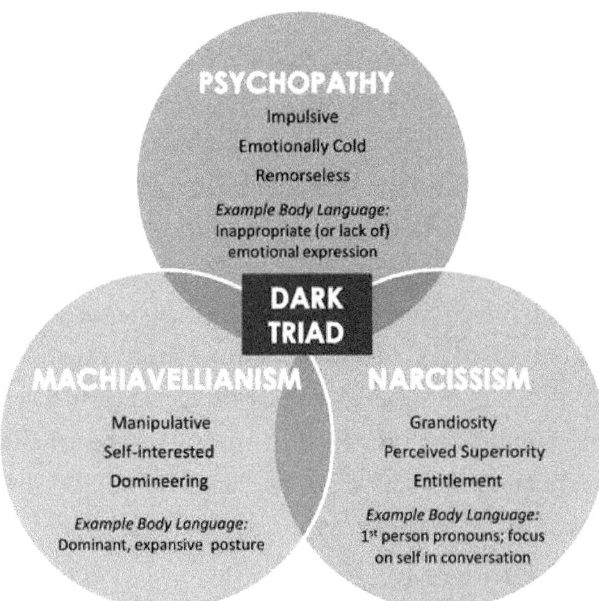

Individuals with high Dark Triad personality traits are often charismatic but highly self-centered, using others for personal gain.

Narcissism: High need for admiration, arrogance and inflated sense of self-importance. **Machiavellianism:** Calculating, deceitful and cynical: skilled at manipulating situations and people to serve their own agenda. **Psychopathy:** Impulsive, thrill seeking, callous behavior, and a profound lack of remorse or guilt. **The Dark Triad** is a psychological framework comprising three socially undesirable and manipulative personality traits: **Narcissism (entitlement/superiority): Machiavellianism (strategic/manipulative)** and subclinical **Psychopathy (lack of empathy/remorse.)**

Here is a list of 10-character traits you will need to walk the path of Lucifer to be wealthy & powerful.

Number One: Can you fake like you care about people and say and do all the right things, but deep down inside you have no connection to their pain, grief, or struggles, and you could care less.

Number Two: You are a master manipulator. You know all the right strings to pull and the right buttons to push. You can use deception to get people to act, think, or believe what you want them to believe. You only focus on your own personal gains and can care less about how other people feel.

Number Three: You have impulsive behavior and are irresponsible. You will never admit to your mistakes. In fact, whoever points out your flaws, you will gaslight them and accuse them of the very things you are!

Number Four: You consider yourself more intelligent, more valuable, and more powerful than anyone else. You believe the world revolves around you. Everyone needs to bow down to you because you think you are more valuable than anyone else.

Number Five: You are addicted to lying and not telling the truth. You have mastered it to an art where you start to believe in your own lies. In fact, your whole life is built on lies upon lies upon even more lies.

Number Six: You are usually very charming and have an attractive personality. You have no sense of embarrassment, which can be seen as a high level of confidence and self-esteem.

Number Seven: You have a lack of remorse. You never feel guilty for the act of pain and suffering you inflict on others. You never hold yourself accountable for other people's feelings or well-being. If you scam them or rip them off it is their fault for being gullible.

Number Eight: You have an exaggerated need for rushed adrenaline activities. You get bored very easily.

Number Nine: You are a natural bully. You bully those that you can use the most as well as bully those you have no use for just because you can. This includes women, children, elderly, and animals. No one is immune to your demeaning harsh words and violent physical outbursts and threats

Number Ten: You have an excessive need to wield power and control over others. You are a control freak, and everything must go your way.

Follow the path of Lucifer. It is possible that you can be rich beyond your wildest dreams. But with it comes a very valuable price that you must pay. The devil promises you the world but gives you nothing in return. It is all an illusion. Wherever you go, you take you with you. Surrounding yourself with beautiful things does not take your ugliness away. You can be lonely in a big luxurious house just as if it were sleeping on somebody's couch. You will not be able to trust others ever again for fear of them taking what you acquired. Living in fear is the lowest level of consciousness you can descend to. This is how addicts are created. The things you possess will eventually start possessing you.

Don't fret. There is another way for those of you that do not want to follow the path of the devil. The path of the Heart goes against the programming of your Matrix. It requires extreme courage and bravery as you must take a leap of faith without hesitation at any given moment.

These are the 10 steps towards prosperity following the path of the Heart.

Number One: You must learn to listen, follow, and trust your heart. Your mind that has been programmed by demons to throw every distraction at you based in fear. Pay attention to your heart no matter what the illusion is showing and telling you. You must not get distracted. Quiet your mind so that you can hear your heart's intelligence whisper to you. Slow is smooth. Smooth is fast. Be patient as you must pay conscience. When the time is right the heart will give you instructions. At that time, you will fearlessly take your leap of faith. The best form of hustling is sitting still.

Number Two: Your ego screams at you, but your heart whispers. The ego will make you doubt yourself by feeding your fears and insecurities. This is your ego. Do not pay attention to it. Its sole purpose is to convince you that the negative voice in your head is you, but it is not. Ignore it at all costs.

Number Three: There are two paths to obtaining money in your world. But both paths have one thing in common that is absolutely required. You must be willing to die for your dreams to come true. If you are a coward, turn back now because you will be wasting your time and energy if you are not ready to put everything on the line. The Matrix requires death as a prerequisite to manifestation. In antiquity it was an animal sacrifice. In modern secret societies, it is children. But for you it can be your cells that need to die to build stronger muscles or lose weight. To manifest money requires the old you to die so the new you can match the frequency your success requires. Either way death is certain.

Number Four: If your mother had you through a natural childbirth, you came into this world headfirst. This is what is required for you to give birth to your dreams. They must come out headfirst. Meaning, you can't tiptoe or try to play it safe. You will fail. You must be aligned when you take that leap of faith. No fear, no turning back, no second thoughts. Going in headfirst is a requirement for manifestation in the Matrix!

Number Five: Symbols and images speak directly to your subconscious. Your subconscious mind is 100% responsible for how you view yourself and the world you live in. It is very important to surround yourself with the symbols and images that support the dream life you want to manifest not to support other people's dreams through your time and energy. Eliminate the images and symbols that do not support your dreams. This includes logos, name brands and the like.

Number Six: Fall in love with the struggle. You are going to go through some hard and painful times. This is a requirement. This is law. Learn to embrace these situations and know that when they finally subside, you will be one step closer to your dreams. Stay in a constant state of gratitude even during the storm. This is very important. Emotions of gratitude and appreciation act like fertilizer to the seed you planted in your subconscious mind that you want to manifest.

Number Seven: Discipline, focus, and heart. The one thing these words have in common is they all have the root word related to fire! Discipline means to learn in the fire. Focus means to gather the fire in you and direct it to a specific direction and heart is spelled like hearth which is the floor to a fireplace. Fire is your passion. Without extreme amounts of your passion and desire into your dreams, they will never be manifested or sustained. Learn to master the fire that burns in you and direct it to fuel your dreams.

Number Eight: Do not be afraid to change courses on your journey. If you put all you got into following your heart's desires, you will discover a secret, hidden path. Don't hesitate to take this path when it is revealed to you. Even though you can't see where it goes, this is the path your heart leads you to. Jump in headfirst!

Number Nine: Don't be afraid to leave the old you behind with your old friends. Embrace the change and a new way of how you look at things. To live the life of your dreams requires you to leave old ideas and people who don't believe in you behind. Being comfortable stops the manifestation process in the Matrix called Hell.

Number Ten: Always embrace your inner child. They will never lead you astray. There will be times when it will seem like there is no way out. That's when you go deeper within and speak to the only being that knows you the best, your inner child. Some of you have never met them. Call on them to lead you. Trust them and they will never lead you astray.

Point A: Money operates within the sacred feminine frequency and must be honored to have longevity and abundance.

Point B: The goddess Isis is where you get the dollar sign from. It is the spelling of her name with each letter overlapping on each other. $$$$ She must be honored and revered.

Point C: Your moon controls the water on your planet. This is where you get the word money. That's where it has its roots. It's a sacred feminine principle. Honor and study the science of the moon.

Point D: Water is a feminine element. The word currency comes from the water current. Pay homage to the element water!

Point E: A flowchart emphasizes the word flow. How water moves. Move like water.

Point F: The word bank comes from riverbanks. They hold water on the sides of bodies of water.

Point G: The word liquidate comes from the state of water in its natural form. Liquidate your assets (Auset.)

Point H: The word assets come from the Kemetic goddess Auset who represents the sacred feminine. The word income stream comes from a small flowing body of water. Move like water in the divine feminine flow.

Point I: A woman's water must break before she gives birth, symbolizing the importance of water and the feminine principle needed for prosperity, abundance and manifestation in this realm.

THE HEART CAN NEVER BE BROKEN

The myth of heartbreak. I know when we go through a breakup or when a person we love passes away, we feel that achy feeling in our heart. We always say that that person has our heart or they're my heart. We always associate that hurt feeling with your heartbreaking. We hear couples that have been married for 70 years say the husband or the wife passes away and then not soon after that their spouse also passes away. They contribute this phenomenon to a broken heart. A broken heart is just a myth. The heart cannot break it is indestructible. Let me explain. The heart resonates at a frequency of 528mz. This is what we call love frequency. The only thing that can exist in this vibration is healing, nurturing, empathy, compassion, humility and looking out for others ahead of yourself. These are the things that hold the frequency of 528. There is no death or fear. The heart cannot break because the heart was only designed to do one thing, Love. It extends itself unconditionally to support life. It is impossible for the heart to break. What you are feeling is the pain of letting go of the Ego. That pain is your ego dying s an ego death. We invest our egos in our relationships based on the fear of abandonment. We don't base them on unconditional love that resides in the heart. We define ourselves and our environment through our egos as we've been conditioned since birth to think that we are our egos. We are motivated by fear. We are motivated by hate. We are led by low self-esteem and lack of understanding. We avoid embarrassment at all costs. We do not want to be held accountable if it makes us look bad. We always play the victim when things don't go our way. It's that part of you that is breaking not your heart. Sometimes it takes a traumatic situation where someone that you love, someone that you've invested in is torn away from you or they leave you suddenly without you knowing it. That pain you associate with the heart is not, it's an ego death. The ego always must have things in their proper place or it will have a fit. The ego does not live outside of its box. It carries its box wherever it goes and that box imprisons you. You think it protects you from humiliation, fear or embarrassment. You think by carrying the ego around with you in your prison box that people won't judge you harshly. All those things are non-existent, but the ego makes them real. It's the monster in you that tells you that you don't look the part. That you're never good enough. That people despise you. That you're not attractive. That people know you're insecure and stupid. That your insecurities are exposed for all to see. That the voice in your head that's your biggest critic is yours and not your egos. When something that you love or something that you invested suddenly is torn from you that painful feeling is the ego dying. Now the ego must reconstruct how it defines you and the reality you live in. Its world just got exposed and torn to shreds. It must create a new box and that takes time to place you in it to make you comfortable again. On the other hand, the heart only wants to love. The heart only wants to give of itself. Wants to show humility. Wants to die for a Cause greater than itself. Only wants to sacrifice itself, nurture, love, heal, show compassion and have empathy. That's all love can do and that's all contained in the heart. We have been convinced that the heart is weak. That the heart is fragile. That the heart is exposed and vulnerable. The best way to protect the heart is to leave it vulnerable and exposed. The Buddhist has a saying when you're unattached from physical things there is no investment, thus there is no loss. The heart loves unconditionally with no attachment. The heart will love even when someone betrays it. It is the ego that has to step in and say no more. The ego creates a prison that tries to lock your heart away, but your heart only wants to love again. It is impossible to break the heart because it houses the most powerful frequency in the Universe, which is Love. It's God Consciousness that cannot be destroyed. It is the Alpha and the Omega. It's the ego that must be destroyed. What you feel in those desperate times are not the indestructible heart breaking but actually the ego dying.

EPILOGUE

"I know you're out there. I can feel you. You're afraid of us. You're afraid of change. I don't know the future. I didn't come to tell you how this is going to end. I came here to tell you how it's going to begin. I'm going to hang up this phone, and then I'm going to show these people what you don't want them to see. I'm going to show them a world without you. A world without rules and controls, without boundaries or borders. A world where anything is possible. Where we go from here is a choice I leave to you."

-Neo. (The Matrix movie.)

Children of War

We are all prisoners of war. This realm has declared war on the innocence, purity, bravery, vulnerability, curiosity and honesty of a child. All of us came into this realm under the traumatic event of childbirth. They ripped us from the safety of our mother's womb and exposed us to harsh and extreme sounds, lights and cold temperature. We came into this world headfirst, so we have been predisposed and conditioned by fear at the time of our incarnation. The fear of falling, loud noises, extreme temperatures and bright lights. We were programmed from birth to pay attention and exclusively be motivated by fear and not love. A child is the greatest resource in the universe because it's the closest thing to the Most High in the physical dimension. That's why

Lucifer and his Fallen Angels prey on the innocence of children. If they can contaminate a child's innocence, they can prevent that child from reaching Christ Consciousness in its future. They can kill "God" before it has the opportunity to recognize itself. In turn, the child will naturally harm others the way he has been harmed to psychologically gain the power that was brutally taken from him. He now becomes a recruit to Lucifer's Fallen Angels and the vicious cycle of sexual exploitation repeats itself. The Illuminati or the Fallen Angels sexually exploit, abuse and murder children at an alarming rate. Over one million children go missing in the United States every year and no one even bats an eye. Its business as usual as society accepts this tragedy as normal. This is sickening. The Epstein files are in the news and to this date only one woman has been convicted for participating in the largest pedophile ring in the world! Coincidently, there are rumors that she will soon be pardoned! These demons are the most powerful and wealthy white men on the planet. They all have immunity and are celebrated in our culture as people to admire and emulate for their ill-gotten gains. Tell me this dimension isn't Hell! In ancient, European culture all forms of sex were considered normal. The kidnapping and sex with minors are where we get the word, "Mentor." At around 8 years old, one of these rich European white men would go to the poor community and "sponsor" a child until he hit puberty. In other words, they would kidnap these little boys, take them home for the next five years, rape them and then dropped them off when they hit puberty and pick another 8 year old boy to sexually abuse. Even sex with animals was considered normal. As long as the European man was in the dominate position while having sex, all bets were off. This was a normalized sexual deviancy that is true today as it was back then. Now it is done in the dark and not glorified like it was in the past. These rich white men still perform these rituals at the expense of our innocent baby boys and girls. These demons will also rape and torture our innocent children and at the time of their heightened fear and pain harvest a chemical called Adrenochrome that surges in their blood stream. The Illuminati believe this chemical is the secret and lost fountain of youth that ancient mythology speaks of. Children are the least protected demographics in our society, and everyone seems to go about their business and act as if this were normal. It is not! We all need to make a conscious effort to protect our children at all costs. And if no one protected your childhood innocence it's never too late to heal the Inner Child in you. They are waiting for you to remember them and go rescue them from the perpetual trauma you never healed from. You, are their only Savior!

INNER CHILD HEALING MEDITATION

A guided meditation using binaural beats, affirmations and breathing techniques to heal your Inner Child trapped in the Root Chakra (Hell)!
[Can be seen on YouTube: https://www.youtube.com/watch?v=1-ug0zvF5DM]

We need to first address our Root Chakra. Our Root Chakra is our foundation.

Like any structure we can only grow according to the integrity and limits of our foundation.

Your childhood is your foundation.

Any needs that were not met in our childhood become cracks in our structures as adults.

These cracks become exposed and amplified when we step out of our comfort zone.

Our reaction to these moments will trigger us to revert to the age when the crack was originally created.

If that crack is never recognized and repaired, you will forever be frozen in your development.

This will lead you into a perpetual cycle of discontent, as you will self-sabotage and be a perpetual victim of your own demise.

Go back to your childhood and address the traumas and abuses you have suppressed in your subconscious mind.

Your Inner Child is waiting for you to save it. It is you that doesn't recognize their worth.

It's time to listen to your Inner Child and give them a voice they never had.

Instead, you listen to your Ego that lives in perpetual fear and imprisons your Inner Child.

Your Inner Child whispers to you while your Ego screams at you.

Quiet your mind to connect to your Inner Savior.

Your Iner Child deserves to be heard for the first time. You have done it your Ego's way and are still unhappy. Give your Inner Child a chance to show you the way out of this vicious cycle of unfulfillment.

It's time to listen to your Inner Child and give them a voice.

Instead, you choose to listen to your Ego that lives in fear and imprisons your Inner Child.

(Repeat seven times: "I Am The Child Of God And God Is The Child In Me.")

Breathe.

Inhale deeply through the nose and exhale fully through the mouth (Repeat 3X.)

Some of you have never met your Inner Child.

You forgot you have forgotten them and now your Ego has taken their place.

Your Ego has convinced you that it protects you, but it really enslaves you.

This is why you cant seem to get out of your own way.

You made a secret deal with the Devil, that lives in your head rent free.

He screams at you to drown out your Inner Child's plea for help.

Your Ego is highly critical of you to break down your self-esteem and self-worth.

He keeps you motivated by fear so you will never meet your Inner Child.

He sabotages your goals and dreams before you even try to manifest them.

You have failed before you get a chance to start.

But all is not lost!

You have your own personal Savior that's waiting to swoop in and save you!

All you have to do is go back and save him so he can have the opportunity to save you!

You may ask where and how can I find him?

Your Inner Child is located in the deep recesses of your subconscious mind.

The only way to retrieve him is to go back to the time and place the trauma happened in your childhood.

This is where you abandoned him. You thought for safekeeping, but you really imprisoned him and stunted your development and growth.

All you wanted to do was protect them from the pain and trauma you were experiencing in real time.

But days turned into weeks. Weeks turned into months. Months into years until you forgot they even existed.

Slowly, over time your Ego, or the Devil, took over your thoughts and you started to doubt yourself.

It taught you to live in fear, don't trust, have self-doubt and never forgive yourself or others.

It taught you kindness is a weakness, innocence is not safe and vulnerability leads to pain.

There is another voice in your head that will never lead you astray.

But it doesn't yell, scream or have a fit to get your attention.

It whispers between the beats of your heart. So one must be still to get its attention.

It thrives in stillness, sobriety, kindness and peace.

It will always allow you to get the last word. But don't be fooled, pride comes before the fall.

Humble yourself. Lay at it's feet. Listen to the wisdom it gives you. For it will never fail you.

Although it's lessons may bring you pain, you will take one step closer to your dreams!

**Sit still with the voice. Let it guide you for once.
Learn to get out of your own way.**

Understand the concept of hustling while sitting still.

When there seems like there is no way out, that is when you go deeper within. This is where you will find your Inner Savior!

Talk to them. Ask them how you can make them happy. Rekindle their forgotten goals and dreams!

Make them a priority. Do the things they loved to do before the trauma, abuse and abandonment.

Love on them with all your heart and all your soul. Welcome them back in your loving arms and vow that you will never forsake them again.

Be unapologetic about your unconditional love for your Inner Child. Intentionally make them your priority.

Tell them that it wasn't their fault. They were taken advantage of when they should have been protected.

They were preyed upon by people they trusted. The adults in their life failed them. Their innocence betrayed and exploited.

Even though you were too scared to speak up for yourself, your silence was not consent. It was a normal response to severe trauma. It was not your fault.

Forgive yourself.

Also, find the strength to forgive those who harmed and betrayed your innocence.

Forgiveness is for you to lighten your heart so that your Inner Child can finally be free.

Breathe.

Inhale through the nose deeply.

Exhale through the mouth expelling all air out of your lungs.

(Repeat 3X)

INHELL.... EXIT HELL....

(Repeat seven times: "I Am The Child Of God And God Is The Child In Me.")

The God in me sees the God in you........

Find a new (Re)-Lease on Life!!!

Written by TC Carrier

www.ingramcontent.com/pod-product-compliance
Lightning Source LLC
LaVergne TN
LVHW050628100826
845148LV00011B/1784

9780983446293